TALKING VROUZ

Valérie Rouzeau
TALKING VROUZ

৯

Translated by
Susan Wicks

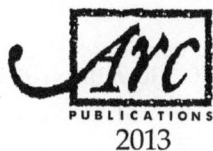

Arc
PUBLICATIONS
2013

Published by Arc Publications
Nanholme Mill, Shaw Wood Road,
Todmorden OL14 6DA, UK
www.arcpublications.co.uk

Design by Tony Ward
Printed by Lightning Source

978 1908376 16 9 (pbk)
978 1908376 17 6 (hbk)

Cover image: Ben Styles

The publishers are grateful to the editors of
the following magazines in which some of these
translated poems have appeared: *Modern Poetry in
Translation; Poetry London; Poetry Review*, and also
to *Poetry International* in Rotterdam, who originally
commissioned and published the translation of the first
four poems.
The author has provided notes at the end of the
book for the sources of her borrowed words where
they are not explicit in the text, which is itself largely
free of italics and quotation marks, and these notes are
attributed and interspersed with the translator's.

'Arc Translations'
Series Editor: Jean Boase-Beier

CONTENTS

PART II:
Poems from
VROUZ

In my introduction to Valérie Rouzeau's first book of poems in English, *Cold Spring in Winter* (2009; originally *Pas revoir* (le dé bleu, 2003)) I have already explained how she and I met in Paris in June 2004 at an international poets' translation workshop where we were set the hugely stimulating challenge of translating one another's poems from French into English or English into French. Even then I think our affinity was perceptible, and when she gave me a copy of *Pas revoir* and I read straight through it the extraordinary – and extraordinarily poetically sophisticated – punch it delivered was impossible to ignore. Since then I have been asked to translate four of the longer poems in her fourteenth free-standing poetry publication and fifth full collection, *Quand Je Me Deux*, for Poetry International in Rotterdam, and I did my best. More recently, with two linked new collections to work from, I've felt less of a professional translator and more of the poet-enthusiast I always was, astonished by how well the laconic, often cryptic procedures of some of the shorter poems work in the original, and tantalised by the conundrum of how they might be translated into my own language. These poems are all about *tone*. And the relationship I feel very lucky to have with Valérie is about tone too – the tone of mutuality and affection set by that first workshop with its expectations of concentrated attention and respect.

The two new books bowled me over. Though their atmosphere is not so obviously one of emotional urgency and, in the case of *Quand Je Me Deux*, in particular, their conception apparently less unified, there was an energy in their language that belonged unmistakably to Valérie Rouzeau and no one else. Her language is a hybrid of liberties and constraints: omissions, grammatical contractions, colloquialisms and archaisms, wordplay, puns and repetitions, childspeak, exploded cliché, and, not least, the heightened awareness of a poetic tradition – French, English and American – in the knowledge of which she writes and against which she places herself.

Quand Je Me Deux was hailed on its appearance by the actor Jacques Bonnaffé with the delighted words, '*Voici du Vrouz!*' Unintimidated, Valérie chose to make *Vrouz* the title of the second volume of her diptych and, following her brave example, it's the word I've chosen to use in my own selection from both books. As a poet, she is truly using language in a very individual way. Yet it seems to me that in translation this language is readily comprehensible to us, here in Britain and surely in other Anglophone countries too.

Preserving the essence of Rouzeau's work in English isn't easy. The challenge here was perhaps even greater than the one I faced when I decided to translate the whole of *Pas revoir*. For me these two newer books clearly asked for a faithful but not totally literal translation. In a poem there are so many meaningful things to be faithful to, and inevitably you have to choose. I chose, firstly, to try and imitate the laconic tone, which seemed to shrug its shoulders at life's baffling juxtapositions in a way I recognized from reading the young Rimbaud, or Boris Vian or, especially, Apollinaire. To keep that in English I felt I needed a rhythm, and my words have been chosen often with rhythmic considerations in mind. Rouzeau's own characteristic telegrammese makes that easier in some ways too: she often suppresses articles, particles, pronouns, auxiliaries, for the sake of fertile ambiguities or sound; she repeats words for pure pleasure, sometimes with a sleight-of-hand change of meaning. She occasionally sprinkles her text with a pinch of English or other foreign words. This gave me a certain flexibility: if I couldn't find an appropriate word with the right syllable-count or stress I could cut a small word or add one – an article, an 'and', a qualifier – perhaps not exactly at the same points that Valérie cut or slipped in her own. Very occasionally in the *Vrouz* poems I've added longer, more significant words. Sometimes, as English, with its compound words, can be almost too succinct, I've needed simply to add metrical weight to a gratuitously short line. '*Une cravate un fil de téléphone*' in

12

'Avaler de tout...' (p. 88), when read traditionally as poetry in French, naturally has ten syllables. 'A tie a phone-flex' has five. So I let myself embroider slightly, allowing the line to become 'A knotted tie a spiral flex of phone' – with Valérie's approval.

While I was translating material from these two books, and especially from the diary-sequence of sonnet-length poems which makes up *Vrouz*, the deeper debate in my mind was about the role and status of the translator of poetry, his or her necessary humility, his or her necessary daring. This time I've stuck my neck out a bit further and begun to think of it not as potential arrogance but as courage. Sometimes perhaps I've stuck out my neck too far, but it was always judiciously, because I thought something more valuable than strict word-for-word accuracy might otherwise be lost. Sometimes it almost seemed that an unknown force had intervened: as I was typing the 'Asters or asterisks' poem (p. 129), my clumsy finger on the keyboard produced 'air-ghostess' and in context it seemed such a felicitous mistake that I laughed aloud. I told Valérie and she laughed too and assured me we should keep this little unplanned child. My translations aren't aiming to take every conceivable precaution! It probably isn't possible – perhaps not even desirable – to be a faultless translator of this material.

That being said, I've been as punctilious and careful as I've been able to, trying for a voice that sounded natural while protecting both the playfulness and the verbal density as much as I could. Some ordinary words can be especially treacherous: sometimes I've translated them without a second thought only later to find myself suspicious that something indefinable has been missed. I look the familiar word up to discover that it does indeed have a second or even a third meaning, and that these obviously contribute to Valérie's text. I can't ignore the surface meaning I first recognised – it's the poem's 'glue'. But the other meanings are both its 'glitter' and its subtext, and without them the poem is diminished. Clichés and idiomatic sayings, like the finally untranslatable *'plancher des vaches'* of

'*Le temps ne passait plus ni la blanquette de veau…*' (p. 114) are 'exploded' into their separate components in a way that revives the dead metaphor, and in an ideal linguistic world the whole procedure would be possible in the target language too. In an ideal linguistic world, the overall meaning (dying) could be honoured, while the cliché's ingredients (cows) were given new, half-humorous savour in the blanquette of veal. But in the real world you have to choose. I tried to change the metaphor entirely (a scrap-yard in the sky?) – but eventually I decided gratefully to call on Shakespeare for help.

These poems are so alive in French – and yet, because my first language is and always will be English, they are not, for me, completely transparent on the page in their French original. I have to work to come close to their cryptic, often many-layered messages, and the natural form of that work takes me back into my own language, where familiarity is freedom and I can be as ingenious and daring as I like. Valérie Rouzeau's poems are not flat on the page. They are true poems, and rewarding. They don't yield their meat readily as her namesake Paul Valéry claimed good prose did, and wither away: there's a performative element, a small girl appearing from behind a curtain to do tricks that make one smile – and it's only later that one realises they were profound. With the *Vrouz* sonnets, and always with Valérie's generous endorsement, it seemed to me to be to be necessary for her English voice to step out from the English chintz and twirl a bit too. It may not work. So many things in the life of a poet don't, as the book shows us, at times painfully. If I've allowed myself more rope here – and there are at least three meanings in my mind as I write that! – it was always for Valérie and the poems' own sake, gambling anyway that this particular game would be worth what she, as the female voice of 'Objection' (p. 52), would call the '*chant d'elle*'.

Susan Wicks

I

Poems from
QUAND JE ME DEUX

ÉDEN, DEUX, TROIS, ÉMOI

I

Le cheval a mangé la rose voice le Prince
Il est ébouriffé il a dû attraper du grand vent comme un arbre et
  des plumes au passage
Montre-moi ta banlieue dit-il et je l'emmène
Voir à meme le bitumen d'une rue pittoresque
Quatre pieds de carottes levés dans le trottoir
Et maintenant allons poursuivre notre fête
Sur le chemin de fer français à cette heure-ci c'est un départ en bleu
Nous nous rendons à pinces dessous le fil à linge où ma jupe
  frissonna il était une fois
(Dans la brise de Praha et puis de Cordoba j'attendais son retour
Je semais en éden béton un jardin pour mieux lui faire la cour)
Alors le bouchon part visant le petit train des mains du bien-
  aimé et je suis très touché

II

(Autrefois à un adieu d'amis je déchire mon vêtement de pluie en
  plongeant d'un mur des Tuileries dans une profondeur grise de
  cypress une nuit et je fais sur mes chaussures un bruit presque
  mélodieux puis j'escalade) je continue sous les étoiles

III

Une file indienne d'Ivoiriens traverse avec chacun sur la tête un
  colis
(Un colis beau colis broccoli)
La cour où la bourrache a levé d'un parpaing creux
(Pour ses yeux c'est fête juste pour ses yeux)
Je veux dire quelque chose de moi à lui et bouleversement
Cette phrase de fourmis noires avec ses pousses de chou vertes
  ou bleues qui se balancent c'est immense aphroparadisiaque
Il n'aura pas besoin de chausser ses lunettes pour lire mon
  amour

EDEN, TWO, THREE AND CHURNED-UP ME

I

The horse has eaten the rose here is the Prince
His hair is all on end he must have met high winds like a tree
    and feathers as he passed
Show me your neighbourhood he says and I take him by the hand
And show him right up close the tarmac of a colourful street
Four carrot-tops growing in the pavement
And now let's carry our party on
To French Rail there's a blue train leaving now
We hoof it on our pegs under the clothes-line where upon a time
My skirt once shivered (in the breeze of Praha then of Cordoba I
    awaited his return
Sowing a concrete Eden a garden the better to woo him with)
Then the cork pops out at the little train from the hands of my
    beloved and I'm deeply touched

II

(Back then at a friends' farewell I tore my mac as I plunged from
    a Tuileries wall into a deep grey pit of cypresses one night
    and did it on my shoes with an almost tuneful sound then I
    started to climb) I go on under the stars

III

A single file of men from the Ivory Coast each one with a box on
    his head
(Lovely broccoli in broxes)
The yard where the borage grew in a breeze-block's hollow
(A party for his eyes for his eyes only)
I mean to tell him something of myself and then the other way
    about and upside-down
This black ant sentence with its waving shoots of cabbage green
    or blue's
An aphroparadisiac and huge
He won't have any need to put his glasses on to read my love

IV

A quatre heures du matin sous la lune il sort
En costume d'Adam mon amant va respire la rose
La rose éclose dans la cour grise
A quatre heures nu sous la lune la ville aurait pu le voir avec
    la rose
Alors j'ai grimpé à son cou
Comme un lierre comme trémière
La rose.

IV

At four in the morning under the moon he goes
In his Adam suit my lover goes to smell the rose
The rose that's opened in the courtyard's grey
Four in the morning naked under the moon and all the city could
    have seen him with his rose
Then I climbed to his neck
Like ivy holly
Hock and rose.

¶

L'armoire est vide pas de morts pas de pain
À glace en date de naissance d'aïeule sombre
Comme un immense couffin quoi va partir
Là-dedans si la galère flambe.

L'ivre bateau que ça deviant l'armoire rappelée si soudain
    jusqu'a la mer bleue rouge noire loin –
Draps dépliés toutes voiles hissées
Les fantômes bernés de l'histoire –
Tu penches, la vie
Vers quel infini quell oubli.

La mite a mangé le mouton
Allons
Si l'or vaut moins que le charbon
Scions scions!

L'arrière tante s'est jetée sous un train par amour
Le cœur que j'ignore d'elle
N'arrange à l'intérieur les affaires personnelles
À ta vie atavisme tata
Sur le quai les métros et l'RER à moi.

Mobilier défermé a perdu son mouchoir
Ses miettes de biscuit lu ses cols roulés troués ses foulards ses
    fichus
Corniche quelle proue si l'on si juche émue
Il n'y a plus d'oiseau pour siffler dans ce bois.

Chavire en mémoire courte chêne massif lourde armoire
Étagères chositude
Penderie hébétude
Miroir exactitude
Dans sa plus jolie robe elle danse elle a seize ans.

C'était il y a longtemps qu'un ange passe maintenant
(Le meuble de mariée servit à faire du feu sitôt feue tata claire
Fouie sans corsets ni yeux).

¶

The cupboard's bare no skeletons no bread
Passed down from my dark ancestor a mirror dating from her birth
Like a giant Moses basket right about to leave
Inside if the whole crap ship goes up in sudden flames.

What a drunken boat this wardrobe is so suddenly recalled to
    the blue red black sea far away –
Unfolded sheets all sails unfurled
And history's hoodwinked ghosts –
You lean out, life
Towards what infinite and what forgetfulness.

The moths have eaten the sheep's wool
Oh come on
If gold's worth less than coal
Let's saw it saw it down!

My great-great-auntie threw herself under a train for love
The heart I never knew of her
Can't straighten out inside the personal affairs
Of your existence at a visit atavistic auntie
On the station platform or the tube the RER for me.

The unsealed furniture has lost its handkerchief
Its crumbs of *biscuits lu* its roll-necks full of holes its lousy
    scarves fichus
A ledge what prow if you're all washed up and perch there awed
Not a single bird is left to whistle in this wood.

She's sinking the heavy wardrobe of short memory and solid oak
Her shelves and thinginess
Her rail paralysis
Her mirror exactness
In her prettiest dress she's dancing she's sixteen.

It was long ago an angel passing now
(The bridal wardrobe sent to make a blaze as soon as my late
    aunt claire
Buried without corsets and eyes.)

21

TRR...

Pour maman, pour mes sœurs Nathalie et Julie, mes frères Stéphane, Franck, David et Nicolas cette comédie...

Voici d'iliade longtemps j'étais petite enfant
Et je touchais à tout
Alors «la trafiquante» mon père me baptisa
Ou plutôt me rappela.

Avec ce sobriquet
Je devins fière fière fière comme une bougie
Tout s'éclairait même le crapaud pisseur
Caché trrès au fond de mon cœur.

Je trafiquais des éléphants microscopiques
Des fourmis géantes du vrai Moyen-Âge
Aux pattes griffues de griffon
À la crinière de lion
À la queue de poisson
Des balais élastiques une ménagerie tactique.

Trafiquante puisque j'embarquais la porcelaine
Les couteaux-qui-coupent
Les dents de la grand-mère
Et je me rougissais au géranium au chant d'oiseau
Me verdissais en sauterelle m'ébleuissais ciel ciel.

Convoquais la grenouille la tortue la laitue
L'escargot l'escarpin
Volé vermeil talon pas mal
À ma mère elle aussi trafiquée par mes soins
Aiguilles et pommes de pin
Cachous crachats crachin.

Trafiquais encore napperons et mouchoirs
Je brodais me faisais mousser
D'un blaireau singulier sanglier
Mystère pater aux rideaux je grimpais
Là-haut terreur juchée en catastrrophe
Et ciré rose avec tête de minouche.

TRR...

for Mum, for my sisters Nathalie and Julie, my brothers Stéphane, Franck, David and Nicolas, this 'comedy'...

An iliad ago I was a little girl
A finger in every pie
And so my father christened me
'The trafficker' – or he recalled me rather.

And with that moniker
I stood up tall tall tall as a candle flame
And everything lit up even the pissing toad
Trrapped deep inside my heart.

I trafficked microscopic elephants
And giant genuinely medieval ants
With a griffin's grip
A lion's mane
A fish's tail
Elastic brushes household zoo of wiles.

A trafficker I shipped out crockery
And knives-that-cut
And granny's teeth
Smeared my face red with birdsong geranium
Grasshopper green and sky sky-blue.

Summoned the frog and tortoise lettuce
Snail and stolen
Bright-red court-shoe quite attractive heel
From my mother also thanks to me mixed up
With needles pine-cones
Cough-drops spittle rain.

And dealt in doilies hankies
I'd embroidered got myself lathered up
With a wild boar badger brush
Hooked by the Daddy-mystery I'd climb the curtains
Terrrified up there purrched on the very edge
Pink oilcloth with kitten's head.

Je trafiquais idem la soupe c'était trrop louche
Toute cette tignasse d'ange qui y baignait
Avec les cubes en or en soit jeté le sort :
Cours à toutes jambes bouillon
Ou brûle mon pantalon!

Je trafiquais itou les yeux de l'ours ronds ronds
Le chiffon de poupée la passoire l'écumoire
La digitale poison nommée gant-de-renard
Dans l'Angleterre profonde comme les bottes de pluie
Où sautais à pieds joints les bons matins trrempés
Attraper la merveille des nuages de passage
Et changer moi pareil.

Trafiquante solitaire tout au fond du jardin ou le nez dans
    l'armoire
Les parents faisaient «trr... trr... trr...»
C'étaient d'étrranges créatures pApache ma Manche
Je crois que je les aimais bien
Dans ce temps aux couleurs simples élémentaires
Idiotes comme si vraiment le soleil était jaune.

Moi je leur arrivais aux mains grandissais bien
J'allais d'ailleurs de plus en plus loin que le fond du jardin
Que le fond de l'armoire que le fond du vieux puits
Il y avait la lune aussi là dans ma vie
Pas celle que l'on avait marché dessus l'autrre
La rayonnante l'effrayante la secrète Phoebé.

Trr... trr... trr...
Je grillonnais pour porter de la chance
Ou quoi de trrès heureux trrès trrès trrès
Parfois le satellite sélène de la terre me souriait
Alors je m'allumais je me balançais haut
Comme la plus petite araignée qu'autrefois je croyais
Suspendue dans le vide.

I trafficked as well in soup not ladlelike
That floating noodle shock of angels' hair
With its cubes of gold let its die be cast:
Run fast as I can from the boiling pan
With fire in my pants!

Likewise I trafficked in the round round eyes
Of bears the rrag of dolls the colander the slotted spoon
The digitalis poison they call foxglove
In England deep as Wellington boots
Where I'd jump two feet at once good mornings drrenched
With water catch the miracle of passing clouds
And changing me the same.

A lonely dealer at the bottom of the garden or my head inside
    the wardrobe
While my parents rolled their tongues, 'trr... trr...'
They were the strangest creatures my Papache my Mamanche
I think I liked them
In that time of simple silly primaries
As if we really ever had a yellow sun.

And I came into their hands I grew
And what's more soon went farther and farther than the bottom
    of the garden
Than the back of the wardrobe bottom of the well
There was the moon too there in my life
Not the one we trod on the other one
The luminous terrifying secret Phoebe moon.

Trr... trr...   trr... trr...
I chirped like a cricket to bring myself luck
Or whatever was trruly happy trruly trruly
Sometime the satellite Selene of the earth would smile at me
And I'd light up swing out high
Like the smallest spider I used to believe
Suspended in emptiness.

Trr… trr… trr…
Je crayonne je chiffonne
Trr… trr… trr…
Trr… trr… trr...
Je note je grigrillonne
Tant que la vie m'étonne
Trr… trr… trr…

Trr... trr...   trr.. trr...
I scribble I scrunch it up
Trr... trr...   trr... trr...
Trr... trr...   trr... trr...
I note it down I chirrup my magic sounds
As long as the world astounds.
Trr… trr… trr…

JE NE ME TIENS PAS BIEN À CARREAUX

À la mémoire de Fernande Zang

Dorénavant sans ciel avec torchon d'aïeule un fantôme
Un revenant coton autant dire un nuage passé troué
Autant dire que je pleure dans le grand mouchoir que ça devient
Dieu perce rien on sait bien qu'y 'xiste pas guère

Il y a des pâquerettes et du vide en ce morceau de tissu
Un jour fut sur l'épaule de grand-maman jeune femme
Un jour c'est dans le temps d'avant le temps navrant
Je vois des têtes de frères dans les buissons avec épines et
    liserons
Je vois les oreilles du cheval qui dépassent plus loin
La petite sœur boude quelque part dans le trèfle à trois feuilles
    ou sous le hangar en tôle grincheuse
Et moi où ai-je la tête

Pas dans la cuisine avec l'éponge au dos très vert gratteux
Les queues des casseroles comme les oreilles du cheval attention
La lettre du père noël dans le livre aux 365 recettes
La lettre du père fouettard confettis qu'on fit tard
Torchons serviettes coulants les nœuds
Ma caboche pas plus là qu'un canard sous la table encore que
Dans cette mômerie on trouve de tout et de memôire
Alors pourquoi pas sous la table à rallonges des gronde partance

Les canards étaient vrais ou faux
On n'a jamais une tête de trop
Même aux vécés avec les journaux les grillons les étrons
On a rarement une tête sans tronc

Et je ne perdrai pas la main dans ce torchon
Ce linge pas lange quoique
Ça marcherait dans une petite chanson
Une petite chanson domestique de joie dissoluble
Qu'un lange y vole

Torchon dérobé à l'armoire pour mémoire et non
Rectangle de toile qu'on utilise pour essuyer la vaisselle

28

NOT KEEPING MY NOSE CLEAN

i.m. Fernande Zang

From this day on no sky a granny's rag a ghost
A cotton phantom you could say a faded holey cloud
Could call it crying in the great big handkerchief it makes
God can't see through it we all know he didn't never exist

There are daisies and emptiness in this scrap of cloth
One day it graced Gran's shoulder when she was young
The next it's part of the time before the dreadful time
I can see brothers' heads in the bushes with thorns and
    bindweed
And further on I see the horse's ears sticking up
The little sister sulking somewhere in the three-leafed clover or
    under the big shed's growly corrugated roof
And where have I left my head

Not in the kitchen with the scratchy very green-backed sponge
The saucepan-handles like the ears of horses careful how you touch
The father christmas letter in the cookbook recipe a day
The note from father flog we finally made mincemeat of
Rags and napkins slipping like a knot
My headpiece gone as an under-the-table duck
While in this childishness you find it all by heart
So why not under the drop-leaf table while it takes its leaves

The ducks were true or false
And never an unwanted head
Even in the lav with the newspapers crickets bobbing turds
Hardly ever a severed head

And I won't lose my hand in this cloth
This drying-up nappy-it's-not
Though it'd be fine in a song
A little household song of fast-dissolving bliss
For a nappy to flap in

Tea-towel nicked from the cupboard for memory's sake and not
An oblong of fabric you use to wipe the crocks

Serpillière belge ou encore texte écrit sans soin
Et s'il brûle c'est de l'eau dans le gaz

Torchon comme une guitare
Un joli coup, un nénuphar
Une minuscule nappe de fortune
(Le hasard rime avec la lune
Et le violon n'est pas jaloux)

Ceci n'est peut-être pas carrément un poème
Mais je me demandais pourquoi j'avais envolé ce torchon
De l'armoire de grand-mère lorsqu'elle est morte hier
Les motifs n'en sont pas des pâquerettes mais deux canards
Deux gros canards et douze oranges
Qu'elles roulent les oranges qu'ils montent les canards lourds
Au paradis perdu toujours
Parmi les pélicans les grues les pères ubus
Et tout ce que je ne sais plus

Nous sommes les sans ciel nous essuyons
Qu'ils montent l'essentiel les canards aux oranges
À présent je comprends un rien de quelque chose
J'ai subtilisé ce torchon
Pour trouver mes paroles
Je sais que ma grand-mère me pardonne d'être drôle
Avec du machin grave

Elle veut bien que l'on rie de ce qu'elle avait mis
Mémé ses deux maris dans le même caveau dans le même
    infini où elle les rejoignit
Grave c'est tombe outre-Manche prononcé autrement
Je retrouve toute ma tête elle est dans le mouchoir
Le mouchoir de géant le torchon du vieux temps
Et elle tourne sûrement.

Or a Belgian mop a sloppily written text
And if it burns there's water in the gas

A cloth like a guitar
A wonderwipe, a star
Of water-lily tiny impromptu table laid by chance
(Luck rhymes with the radiance
Of moonshine and the violin's not envious)

This may not be exactly what we mean
By poem but I was wondering why I'd whisked this cloth away
From grandma's wardrobe yesterday when she died
The pattern isn't daisies but two ducks
Two big fat ducks twelve oranges
And let them roll the oranges and let the heavy ducks
Rise up for ever to a paradise that's lost
Among the pelicans the cranes the Père Ubus
And everything mislaid with my loose screws

We are the skyless we soak up
Let the essential rise the ducks their oranges
These days I understand a tiny nothing bit of something
I've secreted this
To find my words
I know my gran forgives me my sense of fun
With some serious stuff thrown in

She's glad for us gran to laugh at her for having put
Both of her husbands in the selfsame vault the same infinity
Serious is grave across the Channel differently pronounced
I've found my head again all in one piece it's in the hanky
Giant's hanky tea-towel of time past
And it's turning surely.

¶

pour Crocodile

Notre amitié même sous la pluie battante tu marches encore
Tu ne connais pas jamais
Tu ne sais pas toujours
Tu ne pleures pas tu as une poussière dans l'œil
Comme si le bel aujourd'hui –

Comme si des dames du haut de la montagne regardaient
Le bel aujourd'hui où tout se mélange
Parfums et couleurs dans la grande musique la petite chanson
Il y a des arêtes dans tous les vrais poissons
N'empêche l'oiseau de chanter au bout du pied de l'homme
     heureux tant qu'il peut

Notre amitié tu as une grenouille invisible sur la tête
Tu ne fais pas ton âge
Tu arrives un chien mouillé dans les bras un chat rayé dans la
     gorge
Ta plus longue écharpe traverse l'hiver avec la gelée royale mais les
     abeilles sont menacées et les baleines et les ours blancs
Tu ne mens pas tu respires
Tu as des talents d'éléphant

Notre amitié tu bats la mesure et les œufs en neige
Tu es grande et sérieuse comme une enfant de sept ans même
     si tu as beaucoup plus
Tu as une grenouille invincible sur la tête
Et raison tu ne fais pas ton âge
Dans tous les vrais poissons il y a des arêtes
Comme une poussière dans l'œil comme un nuage qui nage
Le temps brasse papillonne vole aussi bien
Peines joies vont viennent en tourbillonnent

Notre amitié tu perséphones.

¶

for Crocodile

Our friendship in driving rain you still walk on
You don't know never
You don't know all the time
You aren't in tears you've just got something in your eye
As if the jocund day

As if ladies on the mountaintop looked down
Where jocund day stands tiptoe and where everything
Mingles perfumes and colours in the great melody the little song
There are bones in all true fish
Yet the bird sings all the same at the toe of the foot of the happy
    man as long and loudly as he can

Our friendship you've got an unseen frog squatting on your head
You don't look your age
You turn up with a bedraggled dog in your arms a striped cat
    in your throat
Your longest scarf goes through the winter with royal jelly but
    bees are under threat like whales and polar bears
You never lie you breathe
You have elephantine gifts

Our friendship you beat time and eggs to snow
You're big and serious as a child of seven even if you're much
    more
You've got a frog on your head that won't be beaten
That's why you don't look your age
There are bones in all true fish
Like a mote in the eye a cloud that swims
Time breast or butterfly or maybe flies
Pain and delight come go in the flow's cacophony

Our friendship you persephone

¶

Quelque chose est tombé de moi dans l'herbe
Une vieille lubie une alliance plume
Une goutte d'eau salée
La note du plombier

Quelque chose est tombé de moi sur le trottoir
Va savoir quoi comme lambeau de mémoire
Cheveu ténu tiré donc quatre épingles
J'ai perdu minimum quatre épingles

Quelque chose est tombé de moi sous la table
Un ouragan une tuile une catastrophe
Un nénuphar une dent de lait l'espoir
Plus clair un jour d'y voir

Quelque chose a monté de moi sans prévenir
Quelque chose fiche le camp du corps
Et des saisons quelque chose s'évapore
Quelque chose maximum.

TENUOUS

Something fell from me into the grass
An old caprice a feather wedding-ring
Drop of salt water
Invoice from my plumber

Something fell from me on to the pavement
Who knows which shred of memory
Split hair not one out of place all lost
Four hairpins marbles four of them at least

Something fell from me under the table
A tile a hurricane disaster
Water-lily milk-tooth hope
The sharper to see one day

Something went up from me without a warning
Something wants out
Of my body out of the seasons something evaporates
Something most

¶

L'ami qui n'entend plus Purcell où est-il
Où est-il
Pas dans mon œil qui brille

L'amie qui ne voit plus d'étoile
Où est-elle
Pas dans le ciel pas dans le ciel

La note qui ne touche plus l'ami
La lumière l'amie
Mon œil ni mon oreille

La note qui est montée au ciel
La pluie qui exténue le marbre –

La pluie qui exténue le marbre
La note qui est montée au ciel

Mon œil ni mon oreille
La lumière l'amie
La note qui ne touche plus l'ami

Pas dans le ciel pas dans le ciel
Où est-elle
L'amie qui ne voit plus d'étoile

Pas dans mon œil qui brille
Où est-il
L'ami qui n'entend plus Purcell où est-il.

¶

The friend who can't hear Purcell any more where is he now
Where is he
Not in my shining eye

The friend who can no longer see a star
Where is she
Not in the sky the sky

The note that no longer moves the friend
The light the friend
My eye my ear

The note that's risen to the sky
The rain that wears the marble thin

The rain that wears the marble thin
The note that's risen to the sky

My eye my ear
The light the friend
The note that no longer moves the friend

Not in the sky the sky
Where is she
The friend who can no longer see a star

Not in my shining eye
Where is he
The friend who can't hear Purcell any more where is he now

RÉPÉTITION

On ne connaît pas le cœur des gens
Il est tant mal visible que parfois
On cogne dedans
Quelle misère de prendre le train
Quand au bout il n'y a personne rien
On ne sait pas l'avis des anges
Non plus que des moulins à eau
On se sert un grand verre de vent
De source de pluie des yeux
On ignore comment vivre comme eux
On se sert un grand verre de vin
Dans une maison avec enfants avenir chien
Le quai fait des bruits de chaussures
Le quai fait des bruits de valises à roulettes et des bruits
    d'avant
Le quai est vide vide vide on bute dans l'air
Pardon messieurs dames j'ai cru à un nuage
Vous êtes innombrables qui ne m'êtes personne
Je suis innombrable et comme vous presque rien
Prenons donc un pot amical au lieu d'un pot au noir d'un
    mauvais coup
On ne connaît pas d'autre cœur dans le noir que le nôtre et
    encore
Ni dans le jour non plus alors à la bonne vôtre
Et nous débarquerons sous le soleil battant.

REHEARSAL

You don't know people's hearts
A heart's so hard to see
That sometimes you bump into it
What a pain to catch the train
When there's no one nothing at the other end
And angels are inscrutable as water-mills
You pour yourself a generous glass of wind
From a bottled spring from rain from eyes
You don't know how to live their kinds of lives
You pour yourself a great big glass of wine
In a house with children future dog
The platform echoes to the sound of feet
The platform echoes to the wheels of cases noises from before
The platform's empty empty empty you stub your toe on air
Excuse me madam sir I thought you were a cloud
You're numberless you're nobody to me
And I am numberless I'm almost nothing as you are
So let's have a friendly drink together no mean tricks no blind
    man's buff
The only heart we know in darkness is our own and hardly even
    that
Or in the daytime either so it's cheers and here's to you your
    good health mate
The sun'll be beating down on us when we step out.

Les corbeaux font croix croix croix croix par-dessus tous mes
vieux sillons
Tous mes vieux cieux délit si eux ils clouent des vœux sans avenir
Ça monte au-dessus du nuage le plus noir qu'on a jamais cru
La ville est froide et le cœur nu
Le sapin brille on l'enguirlande comme il faut une branche morte
Sur la parabole quel oiseau

Mes chemins boueux chemins profonds j'y enfonce un petit soulier
Et il dure jusqu'au macadam où j'ai maintenant les deux pieds
Quelque chose cloche ou boite à vide
Manque la neige l'élément heureux sans paternel sempiternel
La neige et puis ensuite le boueux l'avant printemps le presque bleu
L'empreinte fauvette de joie peut-être

La route du berceau à la tombe offre quelques méchants cailloux
Des blessants cailloux par milliers
Qui n'oublient nos petits souliers
De la poussette au tumulus du joli lange au cumulus
De la laine du mouton au marbre au dernier souffle évaporé
Nous ne savons pas ce que c'est.

The crows go cross cross cross across my old furrowed field
My old delightful skies a crime for them to nail their futureless
    wishes there
It rises above the blackest cloud you ever believed
The town is cold the heart is bare
The fir-tree shines they decorate it as befits a branch that's dead
And on the satellite dish what parable of bird.

My muddy paths my sunken paths my little shoe sinks in
And lasts until the tarmac where I've got two feet again
Something is stumbling limping running on empty
No happy element no snow no everlasting father
Snow and after that the mud the early spring the almost blue
Perhaps the warbler-footprint of delight.

The road from cradle to grave presents a few mean stones
Sharp stones in thousands
That remember all our little shoes
From pram to tumulus from dainty baby-wrap to cumulus
Sheep's-wool to marble to the last evaporated breath
We don't know what it is.

01 43 15 50 67

pour Fabienne

Quand nous cessâmes de parler il a neigé
Nous avions ri et soupiré comme deux sœurs
Vois-tu ce caribou par ta fenêtre c'est un nuage
Un élan une hermine un petit renard mouvant
Change tout le temps change en ciel ciel
Si la nuit s'étoile elle promet du bleu
As-tu vérifié ourses et cheminées
On devrait voir plus souvent un océan
On devrait du premier coup reconnaître une girafe
Blanc blanc blanc blanc chez toi aussi?
Une pieuvre un poulpe un octopousse encreraient bien
Blanc blanc blanc blanc et sans les yeux rouges du lapin
Ne nous mettons pas en retard l'heure tourne allons
Il y en a à robes à pois d'autres à trapèzes
J'allais oublier
Des choses anciennes flottent à la surface et des nouvelles aussi
Une écumoire une convalescence un joyau
Bijou d'eau dormante c'était le nom d'un chat
Ce fut
Noyau
Les nuages ne miaulent pas les bijoux coulent par contre...
Quand nous a cessé de parler il neigeâmes.

01 43 15 50 67

for Fabienne

By the time we finished talking it has snowed
We'd laughed and sighed like a pair of sisters
Can you see this caribou from your window it's a cloud
A moose an ermine little moving fox
It changes every moment changes to sky-blue sky
If the night has stars in it it's a promise of blue
Have you checked out the chimney-stacks the great she-bears
We ought to see oceans more
We shouldn't need a second glance to make out a giraffe
All white white white white where you are as well?
A squid a cuttlefish an octopus might add a splash of ink
All white white white without red rabbit eyes
We mustn't make each other late time's getting on I'd better go
There are some in dotty frocks and some in geometric shapes
And oh I almost forgot
Old things float up and new ones too
A slotted spoon a convalescence or a precious stone
Jewel of sleeping water there was a cat called that
It was
Drowned jewel
Clouds don't miaow though jewellery can trickle down
When we stopped our oneversation we came down as snow.

SEIZE THE DAY (CARPE DIEM)

pour Susan

Aujourd'hui quatrain deux mille neuf
Sur la petite ville où je gîte
Le soleil brille jusqu'aux poussettes
Les bébés braillent comme des marchandes

Je veux attraper ce dimanche
Entre les mailles de mon filet
Gros poisson d'argent préparé
Ce quatre janvier ruisselant

Cueillir les roses de la vie
Épines écailles ceci cela
Garnir un bouquet chanceuse moi
Au marché marcheuse sans marmaille

Lundi a le temps d'arriver
Et l'eau de couler sous les ponts
Pour l'heure je la mets à bouillir
J'y jette nulle éponge ma dorade.

44

CARPE DIEM

for Susan

Today two thousand nine in four-line verse
Upon the little town wherein I lie
Babies like market traders bawl their wares.
Even at pushchair level the sun shines.

I want to catch this Sunday
Keep it in the meshes of my net,
A giant silver fish cleaned and ready
This fourth of January, dripping wet.

To gather while I may life's roses
Thorns or scales a bit of that and this
To garnish lucky me a bunch of flowers
Strolling the stalls and holders strollerless.

Monday can take its time in coming
Water running under each bridge away.
For now I pour it bring it to a simmer
Throw in no sponges my sea bream today.

18 VERS QUOI

«J'euh…»
ANTOINE EMAZ

Je monte et je descends comme la température
Une bonne affaire du temps saison saison saison
Une histoire de saison pluie soleil lune mercure
Je descends comme très enrubannée la toute petite voiture
D'Arthur Arthur Arthur
Et je monte au créneau ou laisse tomber la neige
Effeuille l'éphéméride ça passe et fait mes rides
Regarde la tite auto elle a disparu toute
On ne voit plus son dos on ne voit plus celui de l'âne dessus la
    route
On ne voit plus la route et il faut continuer
À pied à pied à pied
Se distraire chaussure rouge à gauche ou verte à droite
Surtout lorsque l'hiver donne son mauvais tuyau
Sa blague pas drôle de verglas glas sa vieille messe basse
J'on monte et j'on descend sans narcisses ni jonquilles
Ou bien avec selon les astres et les désastres
Le paradis est très perdu d'où l'on nous chasse
Allons allons mouvons.

18 LINES TO WHAT

"I um..."
    Antoine Emaz

I rise and fall as the temperature does
Today's good deal the season season season
Seasonal story rain sun mercury moon
I bring down all done up as if in ribbons
Arthur Arthur Arthur's little car
And climb the time-slot ramparts sprinkle snow
Tear off another page time passes and I age
Look down at the tiny car it's completely gone
You can't see its back you can't see the back of the donkey on
    the road
You can't see the road itself now and we must go on
On foot on foot on foot
Distract ourselves a red shoe on the left or a green one on the right
Especially when the winter plays its rotten trick with pipes
Its flattest blackest joke about black ice its old low mass
I you go up go down without an arse is us without a daffodil
Or with according to predictions astral or disastral
Come on come on let's move
The paradise we're being ousted from is very lost.

VAIN POÈME

L'homme qui portait des gants très jolis hier soir
Mieux que cela : d'élégants gants
Cet homme m'a touchée tant ses yeux étaient grands

Hier soir il pleuvait interminablement ses yeux bleus
Ses yeux gris ses yeux immenses comme il pleuvait
Sur ses élégants gants en laine de mouton rouge et or vraiment

Quand quand va-t-il m'apercevoir je me suis demandé parce que
Tant ses yeux étaient grands et moi tout près
À une flaque de la taille d'une soucoupe d'une étoile

Un piano s'envolait d'une fenêtre au-dessus de nos têtes
Un ovni si ça se trouve c'était peut-être la cause
Qu'il ne me voyait pas alors que moi sur le bout des doigts

Averse à la moi là renverse comme des soucoupes
Il avait les yeux grands
Le piano aqueux je l'ai presque inventé par une fenêtre allumée

J'ai pu distinguer le rouge et l'or des gants ailés gants de lui mieux
Sous l'incessante pluie d'hier douce à la volée
Les couleurs de l'oiseau qui renaît de ses cendres

Qui court qui court qui court sur les touches du piano
Juste une flaque à sauter et je pourrais toucher
Au lieu de n'avoir rien que deux yeux pour pleurer

Les doigts en rouge et or je pourrais m'hasarder
À caresser la laine de mouton ah bergère
Oh Tour Eiffel et s'il l'escaladait

N'est-ce pas Guillaume que de là-haut il me verrait
Au bord de la flaque où flamberait la lune ronde
Où je pianoterais aussi bien que la pluie.

VAIN POEM

The man last night who wore such classy gloves
Or better than that: such glovely gloves
That man touched me with the hugeness of his eyes

Yesterday evening rain without a break his eyes
Were blue were grey enormous as it rained
On his glovely sheep's-wool gloves I tell you red and gold

When when will he notice me I asked myself because
His eyes were so so big and me so close
With only a puddle between us big as a saucer big as a star

A piano was flying out of a window above our heads
A UFO if they exist that may be why
he didn't see me there while on my fingertips

a cold wet downpour pours its saucers down
on that me there. His eyes were big. The watery piano
I almost invented it through a window's light

I could see the red and gold of those winged gloves his gloves
more clearly scattering in yesterday's incessant gentle rain
the colours of a bird that dies and rises from its ash

to run run run across the piano keys
just a puddle to jump over and I could touch
instead of having nothing but two eyes to cry

Fingers of red and gold I could risk a stroke
of that soft wool the sheep the shepherdess
Oh Eiffel Tower if he were to climb

he'd see me wouldn't he Guillaume from high up there
at the puddle's edge where the round moon would flame
and I could let my fingers play as sweetly as the rain

LE POÈME POUR JACQUES

Le poème pour Jacques n'existe pas encore
Il y faut promesse de légèreté
Il y faut liesse aussi de penser
Une plume d'oie rêvée au clavier
Une bonne boîte pour sortir
Jacques-from-the-box rire
Le poème pour Jacques commence
Par cœur finit parce que

Le poème pour Jacques est un poème
Pour Pierre et Paul aussi
Et pourtant non
Le poème pour Jacques n'appartient qu'à lui
Idéalement il vole il subtilise
Il dégage perspectives
Il aime il joue il brise
Fiche le camp s'éternise

Lui faut pas de lésine pas de messe-qui-ne-rie
Que voyage la voyelle au-delà des nues
Avec les hélicoptères les grandes grues
Il lui faut la chance d'un petit bonheur
Ou une vraie joie désespérante
Comme une tour abolie bien sûr la plus haute
Comme quoi
Soulève sous le vent une aile au-dessus puis deux du monde vieux

Le poème pour Jacques fait le clown un peu
L'auguste ou le blanc
Selon l'air du temps
Il lui faut une figure de fête
Tête de litote va va va va
Oublie la rime plate et décoche
Un trait d'esprit une flèche zaoum
Jusqu'au ciel insensible car quoi.

THE POEM FOR JACQUES

The poem for Jacques does not exist as yet
It needs the likelihood of something light
It needs the joy of thought
A goose-feather dreamed up in a keyboard dream
A good club to go clubbing in
A Jack-outside-the-box a laugh
The poem for Jacques begins
By heart and finishes because

The poem for Jacques is a poem
For Peter and Paul as well
And yet it's not
The poem for Jacques belongs to him alone
Ideally steals and spirits things away
It opens up the views
It loves it breaks it plays
It pisses off and yet for ever stays

No room for pettiness no not-a-laughing-Mass
Let vowels voyage out beyond the clouds
With helicopters giant cranes
He needs the chance of a small happiness
Or else a really piercing joy despair
Like a ruined tower the tallest one of course
Like what
Might lift a wing in wind then two above a world that's old

The poem for Jacques can play the clown a bit
The 'auguste' or the 'white'
According to the date and circumstance
He needs a party face
Lightotes-head Vava go go
Forget flat rhyme let fly
A dart of wit an arrow Zaoummm
Into the unresponsive sky a-quiver why.

OBJECTION: A LOVE POME POUR 2 VOIX
(poème interminable)

Vieil amant mal aux dents mal au dos pas cadeau déglingue sûre si ça
dure rends-toi compte : no future

Quel présent quel dingue don maintenant profitons!

Profiteroles le temps vole force coule et tout croule

Course folle vent roucoule cailloux roulent faire est foule

Foule de quoi secoue lance ses dés ou ses osselets avant toi m'en irai
c'est dans l'ordre des choses je vais mourir d'abord

Tu vas m'ouvrir d'accord comme Nerval en verlan ou William
en longs vers si j'expire la première cela peut arriver
accident de vélo broyé contre un pommier une voiture
dans platane l'avion qui tombe à l'eau le bateau chaviré
une balle perdue ronde ronde au fond du pré carré ou dans
quelle avenue de grande ville allumée et le cœur tiens qui
stoppe d'un coup sans prévenir

Quelle improbablité tu me déraisonnes là : le temps sapera tout

Le temps passera c'est tout mais nous en connaîtrons l'or et
l'ores et déjà

L'or et l'or et l'ordure… Il ne faut pas rêver.

Mais tu n'es pas un rêve si l'amour s'invente bel

L'amour s'évente et bien, entends ce que je dis, je désire hiver calme
pas retraite aux flambeaux lune de miel sur les flots et gondoles à
Venise je veux finir en paix

Accorde-nous une chance vivons au jour le jour notre histoire
à la joie

Le ménage la routine casseroles et serpillières balais torchons
serviettes éponges plonges piles d'assiettes nous auront à l'usure

OBJECTION: POÈME D'AMOUR FOR 2 VOICES
(interminable poem)

Old love old toothache backache empty hands old wreck if it goes on look
  here: we've aucun avenir

But what a present what a crazy gift trala so why not profit from it?

Profiteroles time passes lapses everything collapses

All a mad rush the cooing of the wind the rolling pebbles cheek by
  jowl in fair and fowl

A very crowded fair that shakes and throws its dice its knucklebones I'll
  leave before you it's the way of things and yet before I do I'll die

So do or die okay you'll cut me open wide like Nerval in Verlan or
  William in long lines but what if I die first could happen accident
  my push-bike crushed against an apple-tree a car against a plane
  the falling plane engulfed by water boat capsized a drunken round
  of bullets wasted drunk and wasted deep in some square field or in
  what lit-up city avenue and then the well I never heart no warning
  stopping just like that

But how unlikely now you're talking nonsense: time will pull the stops out
  one by one

Time will pass that's all we'll know its gold its gone already old

There's gold and gold and mould... We mustn't dream

But you're no dream if love invents itself this well

And truly love has spent itself oh well please hear me when I tell you I
  desire the calm of winter not a torchlit carnival parade a honeymoon at
  sea Venetian gondolas I want to end in peace

Give us a chance let's take it one day at a time our story of delight

The round of chores routine the pans and mops and brushes dusters
  towels washing-up the piles of plates will wear us to a thread

Manège cocasse tournis tes baisers me transportent soucoupes
fusées ovnis!

Tu n'y penses pas vraiment?!

Mais que si! Songe à la poésie!

*Justement elle est cuite d'avance la poésie en faitouts en marmites
cocottes et poêles à frire!*

Je reconnais l'oiseau son refrain seriné sa façon de vous dire
qu'il ne s'en laisse conter...

Je hais la poésie

Moi non plus souviens-toi c'est pourquoi aujourd'hui je te vole
dans les plumes

Et te prête ma lume

Ta lume au clair de quoi je t'écrirais un doux billet dessous la
lune: es-tu l'ami Pierrot ?

*Ma lume de vieux mec assagi aguerri mon éclairage que tu voies mieux
les choses en face...*

Flamme ferait pas l'affaire en matière de lumière que tu me
donnerais au lieu de prêter pingre?

Tu ne veux rien entendre de ce que j'argumente!

Et toi donc si tu défermais tes écoutilles!

Tu me flûtes romance tu me sonnes de ces cloches et bientôt glas glas glas!

Port nawak je te parle de vie pas de trépas tu ne me comprends
pas ou alors de travers...

A funny roundabout I'm dizzy with your kisses flying saucers rockets ufos taking off!

Surely you wouldn't want?

Oh yes I do! The poetry! Just think!

Exactly. Poetry's kaput it's cooked its goose before we even start in stew-pots stock-pots casseroles and pans of spitting fat!

I recognize the bird its trilled refrain its way of telling you it won't be taken in

It's poetry I hate

I'm with you there remember that's the reason why today I'm pouncing on you all my plumes in flight

I'm lending you my light

Your light by which I'd write you gentle love-notes under the moon: who are you? – friend Pierrot?

My light the light of an old guy who's battle-weary wiser and my light will make you see things as they are…

So when it comes to light a flame wouldn't be right you might have liked to give it to me not just lend it you're so tight

You won't hear any of my reasoning!

And what about you then your ears need washing out!

You trill me a romance you ring these bells at me and they toll bong bong bong!

Whatever, this is life I'm talking of not death you just don't get it or you get it wrong…

Clownette tu m'exaspères

J'essaye tout simplement d'un peu te dérider t'amuser te
distraire!

Là tu me désespères!

Alors tu me laisses comme tomber en amour seule?

Je ne peux pas te suivre tu divagues tu es ivre

Je refuse ton refus toi aussi tu as bu

Mais j'ai de la distance j'ai quand même l'expérience

Ah d'accord et moi presque j'aurais de l'innocence!

Je n'ai jamais dit ça

Tu as dit quoi tu as dis-moi songé à quoi?

Nulle Nuit d'été désormais me transformera

Suis pas une fée je ne m'appelle pas Titania mais garde ta
bougie c'est chant d'elle chant de moi je m'en va je m'en
va...

My little clown you're driving me insane

I'm only trying to amuse you lighten you up a bit and wipe
away your frown!

Now I've no hope left!

So what it comes to is I'm left to fall in love alone?

You've lost me now you're wandering you're drunk

I won't take your refusal you've been drinking too

But I've got distance all the same I've got experience

Oh right and I've got almost innocence!

I never said

What did you say just tell me what were you thinking of?

No summer night can change me now

I'm not a fairy my name's not Titania but keep the candle keep
my can delight my song you can't delete I'm out of here I go
I go I'm out...

TRENTE-DEUX DENTS

pour Anne, pour mon frère Franck

Ne loue pas de camion je vais te transporter
J'ai un petit fourgon tes affaires y tiendront
Souris tu déménages tu vas vers nouveaux jours
Qui sait nouvel amour
As du champ devant toi toutes tes dents tes deux bras

Tes deux yeux tes dix doigts ta caboche têtue
Tu as tout ce qu'il faut un front un dos des pieds
Des milliers des milliards de cheveux oui je veux
Tout ce qu'il faut en somme n'est-ce pas merveilleux
Enfin te voilà toi femme entière accomplie

Femme totale sur sa route c'est un bien crois-moi bien
Une aubaine vois la chance avec toi t'attriste pas
Que ça roule maintenant vale l'hier vale l'avant
Une page se tourne ça doit être légère
Comme avion de papier

Ne te tourmente pas tu es lancée partie
Mords la vie mords la vie mords la vie mords la vie.

THIRTY-TWO TEETH

for Anne, for my brother Franck

Don't rent a lorry I can move your stuff
I've got a little van your things will fit in fine
Smile you're just moving house you're off to better days
New love who knows
And everything to live for both arms all your teeth

Two eyes ten fingers your own stubborn bonce
Everything you need a forehead backbone feet
Thousands of billions of hairs yes yes affairs
Everything you need in fact it's marvellous
Here you are at last a woman you accomplished and complete

A total woman on her way that's great believe me
It's a gift can't you see that luck is on your side
Don't be sad it's okay now outweighs the yesterday before
You're turning the page you've got to make it light
As a paper dart

Don't beat yourself up you're launched already you're in flight
Bite into life bite into life bite into life bite.

CŒURS CROISÉS

Un vrai j'ai rencontré de corazón c'était mon frère
Mon poteau mon amie ma sœur mon étrangère
Aucun prétexte aucun playtex la marque je crois
De vieux soutiens-gorge d'autrefois les cœurs croisés
Hier encore ça palpitait joyeusement
On était à la fête
D'autres fois cogne trop fort l'angoisse despote
Je m'hearttardrai j'espère assez
Tant que ça bat j'ai encore pas sorcière

Quelques choses à faire
Corazón muscle gymnaste quel acrobate
On n'en voit pas la couleur ni le serrement
Et c'est peut-être de la chose âme dont je parle
Plutôt que de courage à traverser une vie
Bon sang de mauvais sang
Frangines frangins je vous ensemble
Dans la pensée le vent où va tout
Je nous.

CROSS MY HEART

I knew a real stout Spanish heart he was my brother
Leaning-post best mate my sister stranger
No excuses hold-ups Playtex that was the make I think
Of those old bras of long ago the cross-your-hearts
Just yesterday it was palpitating gaily
While we lived it up
At other times anxiety plays the despot thumps too loud
I'll heart it out I hope for long enough
As long as it still beats I've still got I'm no rocket scientist

A few things to be done
Gymnastic muscle *corazón* what an acrobat
You can't see its colour or the way it squeezes
And the thing I may be talking about is soul
Rather than courage just to cross a life
Its bloody good bad blood
I you together brothers sisters my old mates
In my thoughts the wind where everything must go
I us.

GUE DIGUE DON
(petite suite télégraphique classique)

1

En douce pente Télégraphe Place des Fêtes Jourdain Pyrénées
Belleville
Un bon vent te pousse une bonne pluie te lave les yeux
C'est le temps qu'il faut pour tourner le dos à l'amour mortel
À l'air libre tu trouves le sens de la marche et tu vas –
Sous tes pieds le métro les morts les musiciens.

2

Les rues sales leurs noms propres
Tu confonds moins deux arbres que les Chinois
Bazars Belleville depuis Télégraphe et via les Pyrénées sans
éléphant la Tour Eiffel
Tu voudrais voir surgir pareil une file de canards en marche
indienne
Mais c'est bientôt Noël tu t'étrennes à mourir comme font les
orphelins
Toutes les oies au ciel tu parles
Un nuage sort de ta bouche tu penses à Vladimir en pantalon
Mais pas de neige
Pas de bras pas de chocolat.

3

Au solstice d'hiver ta chanson malingre n'enguirlande rien
qu'une ou deux secondes
Ce sont les vieux bonhommes qui dirigent le vieux monde
depuis trop longtemps
Si tu pouvais déverser dans la hotte de celui-là le gros que tu
as sur la patate
Rigoler comme un vrai ruisseau
Apprendre le russe et le chinois
Compter jusqu'à vingt-deux ou trois
Embrasser qui quoi tu voudras.

GUE DIGUE DON
   (a little telegraphic sequence in the classical manner)

   1

Down a gentle slope from Télégraphe to Place des Fêtes Jourdain
   to Pyrénées Belleville
A good wind fills your sails a good rain bathes your eyes
It's the weather you need to turn your back on mortal love
In the free air you find where walking leads
Under your feet the underground the dead the buskers with their
   instruments.

   2

The sordid streets their very proper names
You can tell the trees apart more easily than two Chinese
Bazars Belleville from Télégraphe and through the Pyrenees
   without an elephant the Eiffel Tower
You'd like to see them all come up for air like a line of waddling ducks
But soon it will be Christmas you've had it up to here with
   treating yourself to things like an orphan
Tell me about it all the geese in the sky
A cloud comes out of your mouth you think of Vladimir in his trousers
But no snow
No arms no chocolate.

   3

At the winter solstice your thin song's a two-second paper-chain
Old farts have been in charge of this old world for far too long
If you could just throw up in that one's sack the big lump on your
   chest
Chuckle like a mountain stream
Learn Russian and Chinese
Count up to twenty-two or three
Kiss who or what you want.

4

Loin (tu frôles les vitrines) l'étang rempli de tes cailloux
(Les dragons de résine) la grenouille qui ne veut pas mourir
Feu craché à la Seine à la Sauldre à moi
Ce mille mètres tout s'y mélange
Un poisson brille sans tête (et l'histoire te rattrape) station
    Jourdain
Tu passes ton chemin d'asphalte tu y vas bien
Pour un peu dans sept jours tu carillonnerais.

5

Pigeons au sol grouillent comme pintades
Au ciel blanc l'avion invisible tu y es presque
Où tu voudras quand tu voudras
Tu connais la chanson maintenant tu iras
Pour commencer sus au tas de pingeons
Tu fonces gagnes deux foulées
À tribord la rue des Solitaires et toujours tout droit la mer.

6

Ci gire le refrain des amants quelle bonne révolution vas prendre
On dirait qu'il a plu ta vie quitte ton ciré arrête ton char plein
    de canards et de pingouins
Prends-toi une année rhétorique lunatique panoramistique
Pose bonne distance pied de travers pied de la lettre et courant
    d'air
Mesure ta chance
Ne retiens rien.

4

Far away (you rub your nose against the glass displays) the pond
    full of your stones
(The plastic dragons) frog that doesn't want to die
They spit their fire in the Seine the Sauldre on me
These thousand metres everything mixed up
A headless fish shines out (and history catches up) at Jourdain
    station
You go on your asphalt way you're doing fine
A week from now it wouldn't take much to make you ring out chimes.

5

The ground is crawling with pigeons like guinea-fowl
In the white sky the plane's invisible you're almost there
Where you'll want to be and when you want
You know the song and now you'll go
To begin with death to the pile of pidgewins
You hurry two strides closer than you were
To starboard rue des Solitaires and still straight on the sea.

6

Here flies gyrating the refrain of lovers what a revolution you can take
You'd think it had been raining on your life slip off your mac and
    bring your cart of ducks and penguins to a stop
Take a year out a rhetorical take a lunatical a panoramystical
Get some perspective a wrong-footed footing a breath of fresh air
    in the literal
Weigh up your luck
Don't hold on don't hold back.

7

Le jeune homme son vieux prénom
Il mange une pomme
On descend tous d'Avant et Ed contrepète maman
Le jeune homme son vieux prénom
Oh monde quelle histoire amour quelle épicerie.

8

Les guirlandes et le bœuf et l'âme
Petits Roms à toute vitesse courent où
Tu te demandes s'il existe la bonne année du chien toi tu es chèvre
Et que deviennent les moutons alors kebab aspirateur?
Tu mélanges tout tout tourbillonne
C'était peut-être seulement la réalité et maintenant
Tu crois que l'enfant si on ne l'achète ni ne le vend l'enfant
    aussi va trouver un jour de l'inconnu
Il faut partir à présent dépêche-toi
Où crèche-t-il ce gamin devant glisse-t-il ses menottes dans
    sa boîte en fer sébile manchon manchon sébile sébile
    manchon pour s'endormir au creux d'hiver au cœur du
    froid.

9

Tu marches à la mort penses-tu
Mais c'est tout le monde et quand même eusses-tu mis des
    dim-up
(Ça te ferait à défaut d'une belle jambe une grande chaussette
    pour le pied du sapin)
Et puis comme Gaston tu marches à l'amour aussi bien alors
    va
Absente perds et trouve toi.

7

The young man and his old first name
He's eating an apple
We all come down from Advent and Ever After, spoonerises Mum
The young man his old name
Oh world what a story love what a corner shop.

8

The paper-chains and ox and Mass
Little Roms at top speed are running where
You wonder if it exists the happy new year of the dog you're goat
And what becomes of the lambs well vacuum lamb kebab
You mix it all up and everything whirls round
Perhaps that was only what was real and now
You think the child if you don't buy or sell it will one day discover
    something unknown too
We've got to leave now hurry up
Where does he crèche this kid before us does he slip his handcuffs
    in his tin his begging bowl his muff his muff his bowl his bowl
    his muff to go to sleep in deep mid-winter in the heart of cold.

9

You walk towards death you think
But everyone does that and even if you'd worn your hold-up
    tights
(If not a lovely leg they'd have made a great big stocking for the
    tree)
And then like Gaston you could just as well be walking towards
    love so go
And in your absence lose yourself and find.

¶

Et je me demandais quel oiseau pourrait bien
Me prêter une plume pour écrire comme avant
Avec de l'encre noire sur du papier bien blanc
La poule la poule grégaire ne fera pas l'affaire

Mais la poule qui gratte au beau milieu d'un champ
Toute seule avec un songe sans doute beaucoup trop grand
Là de la terre au ciel des vers des rêves de vol
Qui sait ce qu'il y a dans un oiseau parti

Des cailloux des coquilles un certain nombre d'heures
Pas tellement de temps somme toute mais bien assez
Pour traverser un paysage résolument
Jusqu'à sortir du cadre comme une bonne idée
Échapper au cliché et à la poésie
Redevenir une poule nature absolument
Un merveilleux nuage.

¶

And I was wondering what bird might lend
me one of its feathers so I could write as I did before
with good black ink on paper white as white
The chicken clucking in the flock won't do the trick

But the chicken scratching right in the middle of a field
all on its own with a dream that's probably too big
there there from earth and sky the lines of worms the dreams of flight
Who knows what there is in a bird that's gone

Pebbles and shells a certain sum of hours
not that much time when all is said and done but quite enough
to cross a landscape with determination
out beyond the frame like a good idea
escape from cliché poetry
become an ordinary hen again completely
a marvellous cloud

¶

J'ai dû rêver cela
(Mais de quoi les rêves sont-ils faits –
What is the stuff dreams are made of?)
Il tombe du ciel solide comme des bouts de plafond

(Y aurais-je une araignée –
That is a bat in the belfry?)
Un souffle au cœur pour rien?
Pour la mélancolie un petit chien?

Non je ne suis pas folle tout pesé bien
Quand même j'attends en vain –
Nature pas morte still life
De dehors le jour point

Drap sur moi je ne dors pas suis assise
Dans mon cauchemar où le monde explosa
Et je me métamorphosa
Avec la lumière revenante.

¶

I must have dreamed it
(But what makes up our dreams –
What is the stuff dreams are made of?)
It's raining solid sky like bits of ceiling

(Could I have a spider there –
A bat in my belfry?)
A heart murmur with no basis?
A little dog to ease my sadness?

No I'm not mad when all the evidence is weighed
Even if I wait in vain –
Nature morte is still life still a life
And day breaks from outside

A sheet over me I'm not asleep I sit
In my nightmare where the world exploded
And my I transformed herself
A revenant with the returning light.

II

Poems from
VROUZ

for Christian Bachelin, my dear Tenebros

¶

Bonne qu'à ça ou rien
Je ne sais pas nager pas danser pas conduire
De voiture même petite
Pas coudre pas compter pas me battre pas baiser
Je ne sais pas non plus manger ni cuisiner
(Vais me faire cuire un œuf)
Quant à boire c'est déboires
Mourir impossible présentement
Incapable de jouer ni flûte ni violon dingue
De me coiffer pétard de revendre la mèche
De converser longtemps
De poireauter beaucoup d'attendre un seul enfant
Pas fichue d'interrompre la rumeur qui se prend
Dans mes feuilles de saison.

¶

Et d'aventure ma main
Saurait faire autre chose
Ma tête ne suivrait pas
Elle est remplie de trous
À la cuisine passoire
Couture chas de l'aiguille
Puis mon humeur chameau
Qui trouve tout difficile
Surtout le paradis
Surtout les spaghettis
À la sauce tomate
Mais danser comme un pied
Je peux y arriver
Talon pointe anapeste.

¶

I'm good for this or nothing
Never learnt to swim can't dance can't drive
A single car not even one that's small
Can't sew can't count can't fight can't fuck
Can't master how to eat or cook
(I'll ask someone to scramble me an egg)
And as for drinking that's a real dead loss
But dying is impossible right now
I'm useless on the flute can't ride a hobby horse
Or wow you with my hair can't let it all hang out
Sustain a conversation
Vegetate a lot expect a single child
Not up to interrupting murmurs that run wild
Among my leaves in season.

¶

And if by chance my hand
Were versed in something else
It'd leave my head behind
Shot through with little holes
A kitchen colander
A sewing needle's eye
My camel gets the hump
And finds it all too hard
Above all paradise
Or spaghettini spiced
With pesto portuguaise
But dancing I'm all feet
Heel toe and anapest
I'll get the hang of it.

¶

Aéroport mes chaussures vertes
Délacées et moi en chaussettes
J'ai grimacé dans chaque miroir
À la pointe des pieds coton bleu
Aïe la tremblerie des voyages
Il faudrait ne boire que de l'eau
Ça ferait de meilleurs nuages
Qu'une mauvaise tête dans un hublot
Une méchante tête d'évapeurée
Quelque chose d'international
En petites bouteilles interdites
Au-dessus des profonds poissons
Mal à mon ouïe mal à ma nuque
Je sens pousser mon cœur navré.

¶

Qui donc se rappellera moi
Pas moi pas moi pas moi pas moi
Épicure les piqûres
Au jour le jour des roses
Pétales bien sûr la fleur
Se recueille puis s'oublie
La gamine au fond du jardin
En paix pourrit son lapin
Alors oui saisir ce qui passe
Main tendue vase accroche-cœur
Attraper une crève un train
Se lever de très bonne heure
Ou veiller toute la nuit
De la vie la vie la vie.

¶

Airport my green boots
Unlaced in stocking feet
I've made a face in every passing glass
On tiptoe in blue cotton socks
Yikes I've got the travel shakes
I ought to stick to drinking water
I'd see better clouds
Than this bad portrait in a porthole
Feather-head of fright
Something international
In small forbidden bottles
High over the deep fish
My ears are aching and my nape
And yet I feel my battered heart expand.

¶

Who on earth will remember me
Not me not me not me
So better savour the bouquet
Of barbs the roses day by day
Their petals yes of course the flower
Folds itself together then forgets
The child at the foot of her garden
Peaceably her rabbit rots
So yes catch hold of what goes by
A reaching hand a vase a curl of hair
Or catch a fatal illness catch a train
Let's get up with the dawn
Of life of life of life
Or else sit up and watch away the night.

¶

J'ai rêvé que mentais sur mon tour de poitrine
En disant comme avant mais avant quoi au fait
Bien bien installez-vous sur mon tapis volant
Glousse la gynécologue dans la réalité
Robert et puis Robert ça sonne un peu Dupont
Beaucoup Dupont Dupond mais pas si rigolo
Parce que le cœur battu en a sur lui trop gros
Et je recycle ici l'expression d'un poteau
Belles athlètes aux maillots de couleurs vives battantes
Avec un numéro gagnant à votre buste
Salut à vous toujours lancées toujours partantes
Réveillée merle et zut il faut encore aller
Chercher une ordonnance bonnet blanc blanc bonnet
ABC la culotte pieds dans les étriers.

¶

Il est quelle heure je suis heureuse il y a un arbre
La guerre le nucléaire heureuse il y a un arbre
Ce mille milliardième oiseau éteint un arbre
Une promesse de forêt d'oubli de je m'en vais
Quelle heure du soir comme du matin
Un arbre dressé franc qui remplit mes deux yeux
La page le paysage la fenêtre aussi bien
Un humain par seconde meurt il y a un arbre
Où la fille à l'escarpolette en l'air s'envoie
La joie en quels temps pays de vivre quoi
Il y a un arbre n'empêche pile juste ici
Levant couchant il tient en embranchement
La lune et le soleil le soleil et la lune
Un arbre un arbre voyageur impeccable.

¶

I dreamed I lied about my bust-size
Giving one before before I what in fact
Good good hop up here on my flying carpet
Chuckles my real-life gynecologist
Robert and then Robert it sounds quite like Dupont
A lot like Dupont Dupond but less apt to make you laugh
(It's an old friend's expression I'm recycling here)
You lovely women athletes in your vivid vests
With winning numbers fastened to your chests
Let me salute you always starting from your blocks
The blackbird's woken up and crap I must go back
To pick up a prescription cup of white white cup
Down with the knickers feet in stirrups up.

¶

What time is it I'm happy there's a tree
The war atomic power happy there's a tree
That thousand billionth bird wiped out a tree
The promise of a forest of forgetting of I'm off
What time of evening like what time of morning
Here's a tree straight up and filling both my eyes
The page the landscape or the window you could say
A human being dying every second there's a tree
Where the girl in the swing is swinging herself to air
La joie in what times countries if you like *de vivre*
There is a tree, though, just here right outside
From rise to set its forking lines connect
The moon and sun the sun and moon
A tree that travels perfectly a tree.

¶

Tant de jours engloutis de temps à tout jamais
Perdu irrattrapable et je commence demain
Sans angoisse ni black-out je répare dès demain
La carcasse rosserie la carrosse carrosserie
Et le moteur aussi qu'il fasse son meilleur bruit
De montre bien discrète subtile et régulière
À la place de ces boum boum boum de cœur débile
Cet affolement motif euphorie dysphorie
Affolement émotif parmi la compagnie
Des autres émouvants ma pensée d'éclopée
De la vie mal possible en façon demeurée
Séjournée qui n'avait pas demandé séjour
Voyagée qui voulait rester à la maison
Avec besoin de rien qu'un morceau de fenêtre.

¶

Mangeurs de pommes de terre
Personne ne va au ciel
Ce serait le bouquet's
L'enfer du gratiné
On nous a pas sonnés
Temps compté rolex bling
Dingue dong bling dingue schlingue bling
Faut garder la patate
Au beurre en robe des champs
Purée petit volcan
Sautées comme comme repas
Jours de ceinture serrée
Et pas de jus dedans.

80

¶

So many swallowed days and so much time
Forever irretrievable tomorrow I'll begin
Without anxiety or black-outs I'll repair
The carcass naggery the carriage's incarcery
The engine so it makes its sweetest sound
Discreet and subtle as a well-wound watch
Not this thud-thudding of a laboured heart
This jitter-flutter of euphoria dysphoria
This welter of emotion when in company
Of moving others or my own lame thoughts
Of life that's barely possible like I'm
Retarded I'm arrested I've unwillingly outstayed
My welcome, widely-travelled would-be stay-at-home
Not needing anything except my square of pane.

¶

Us eaters of potaters
No one gets to rise
But would-be take the cakers
Our hell's all browned-off pies

Their rolex ticks its bling
They never asked us our
Ding crazy dong pong bling
Don't lose your vinegar

Long days with tightened belt
A fry-up with no fuss
In jackets butter-melt
A mashed Vesuvius

And not a bit of juice.

¶

Rencontrez l'âme sœur sans payer jusqu'à dimanche
23h59 ensuite c'est impossible
Les coups de minuit sonnent vous rentrez en citrouille
Un pied nu dans le froid de la nuit d'hiver longue
Le temps file ses heures file son vilain chapelet
Ses secondes au galop poussière de sablier
C'est gratuit maintenant sautez sur l'occasion
Ne ratez pas ce coche votre amour vous attend
Vous avez oublié vos code et mot de passe
Célibataire distrait solitaire étourdi
Please please enter your pin votre pine s'il vous plaît
Votre épine dans le pied que vous avez laissé
Aller nu par ce temps 23h59
C'est minute papillon maintenant ou jamais.

¶

Aujourd'hui seize juin deux mille onze
Bloom en trombes de bonne eau du ciel
Ted & Sylvia se remarient
Cinquante-cinq ans qu'ils ont dit oui
Cinq cinq pour une main donnée
À toi with this ring I thee wed
C'est parti pour une épopée
L'amour la vie la poésie
Il y aura des fleurs un renard
Quelques voyages et deux enfants
Puis des lettres d'anniversaire
Il y aura une astrologie
Beaucoup d'étoiles et d'abeilles
Avant l'hiver définitif.

¶

To meet your soulmate without paying afterwards
Till Sunday midnight minus one's impossible
The midnight chimes ring out your pumpkin rolls
You home with one bare foot *exposé* to the cold
Of an endless winter's night. Time's running out
Its nasty rosary its sands its gallop through the dust
And now it's free so let's jump at the chance
Don't miss this coach your love awaits
But code and password have both slipped your mind
You sieve-head singleton you dozy loner
Enter svp your pin your prick oh please
The spine that's in your sole the one you left
To wander bare one minute to in weather
Cold as this. One minute butterfly it's now or never.

¶

Today sixteenth of June two thousand and eleven
Bloom in cats and dogs good water from the sky
Ted and Sylvia get married for a second time
Fifty-five years now since they both said yes
Five-five five-all to give a hand
To you *with this ring I thee wed*
And so the epic tale began
Love life and poetry
There will be flowers there will be a fox
One or two journeys and a brace of kids
Then some birthday letters
There will be horoscopes
A lot of stars and bees
Before the winter that will never now unfreeze.

¶

Je me fiche de perdre mémoire artificielle
Méga giga octets disk dur clef usb
Pour l'autre humaine organique fragile
Je porte le chapeau qui me va
Je ne suis pas au monde (étoile)
En vers marche à l'envers
Me désolidarise et me désactualise
Sors de l'écran dans la rue bruyante
Arbres en ligne platanes à suivre
Pensées ruisselantes clignotantes
Mes syllabes me refont les pieds
Et tous mes souvenirs (étoile)
Je les inventerai (étoile)
Je les inventerai (étoile).

¶

Les mains des jeunes mères sentent l'huile de foie de poisson
L'oxyde de zinc le salicylate de méthyle
L'huile essentielle de géranium la graisse de laine
L'eau purifiée la vaseline le butylhydroxyanisole
En cas d'érythème fessier (fesses rouges) du nourrisson
Elles ne sont pas approximatives elles viennent et vont
Elles prennent très au sérieux la moindre irritation
Parfois elles s'accompagnent d'une petite chanson
Alors elles dansent un peu comme des oiseaux bagués
Font dans l'air des gestes appliqués joyeux
Le bébé rit et pleure à la fois frétille
Ses joues rebondies rougissent à leur tour
Les petits poings les petits pieds s'agitent
Sous les doigts de la mère qui sentent le poisson.

¶

My artificial memory? I couldn't give a toss
Mega giga octets hard disk USB device
As for the other one the human frail organic
I shall wear the hat that suits me best
I am not in the world (a star)
In verse I am inverse
I cut my ties I leave the now extemporise
Exit the screen to meet the noisy street
Trees in a line these planes the line I take
My thoughts are dripping wet flash off and on
My syllables give me new feet again
And all my memories (a star)
I'll make them up (a star)
I'll make them up (a star).

¶

The fingers of young mothers smell of cod liver oil
Zinc oxide methyl salicylate
Essential oil of geranium lanolin
Distilled pure water vaseline butylhydrocyanisol
In case of erythema (nappy rash) in the nursing child
They don't do things by halves pace up and down
The smallest irritation's very serious
Sometimes they set themselves to music with a little song
And then they dance a bit like ring-tagged birds
Make studied joyful gestures in the air
The baby laughs and cries at once and squirms
Its round cheeks blazing now as red as hers
The little fists are pumping and the little feet
Under the mother's hands that smell of fish.

¶

J'ai chu dans la neige l'autre jour
Après le Café Rouge fins vins
Sic mais pas sick juste étourdie
Sur le cul que j'ai rebondi
Un ange est passé juste après
Ma glissade sous le ciel blanchi
Ensuite un ramier a claqué
Très fort des ailes j'ai sursauté
Comme s'il avait giflé ma joue
Rompu ma minute de silence
Pour me réveiller d'un seul coup
Alors me suis remise sur pieds
Avec un flocon sur le nez
Le rire de l'ange et du ramier.

¶

Négatif je ne sais pas photographier non
Je devrais peut-être m'offrir un téléphone
Il neige et je regarde tomber la neige
D'un œil ni argentique un œil ni numérique
Nul désir de mettre en boîte je n'ai
Une telle magie mouvante nul arrêt sur l'image
Ne ferait voir ma neige sa féerie son appel
Même si ici c'est encore un cliché que j'écris
Magie féerie quelques syllabes pauvres flocons
Si encore je les attrapais en tourbillon
De joie vrouz avant que mon cœur fond
Comme un renard un hibou une hermine
Beaux animaux variables de l'été à l'hiver
De l'hiver à l'été mes bêtes imprenables.

¶

I measured my length the other day in snow
After the Café Rouge *fins vins*
Sic though not sick just miles away
I fell and bounced up on my arse
Just after I had done my slip-and-slither
Under the faded sky an angel passed
A wood-pigeon clapped its wings together
Very loudly made me start
Like it had slapped me on the cheek
Broken my minute's silence from above
To wake me instantly
And so once more I stumbled to my feet
With a snowflake on my nose
Greeted by laughter from the angel and the dove.

¶

Negative I don't know how to take a photo no
Perhaps I ought to buy myself a phone
It's snowing and I watch the snowflakes fall
With an eye that's neither digital nor silvered
No desire to put things in a box I've no
Such moving magic no fix on the image no freeze-frame
I couldn't demonstrate my snow its mesmerising spell
Even if it is another cliché that I write
Like magical enchantment a few syllables poor flakes
If I could only catch them in a whirlwind
Of authentic *vrouz* delight before my heart should melt
Like a fox an owl an ermine lovely creatures
That transform themselves from summer into winter
Winter into summer beasts that can't be caught.

¶

Elle est inconnue remet sa boucle d'oreille
Une feuille court le vent devant elle vole
Sur la longue avenue chacun chacune s'arrange
Couleurs parfums tissus de quoi se distinguer
Ou simplement dehors aller par tous les temps
Comprendre plus ou moins le monde et soi
Un nuage nucléaire une odeur de jasmin
La pleine lune tout au fond d'une journée de pluie
Trace marronnasse de merde au jean d'un homme hagard
Privé depuis des lustres de pain de toit de cul
D'amour tout court il a dû trébucher rater
Une marche ou un virage un passage obligé
Au moment où elle repart que l'arbre est nu
Nombreusement planté au bord de l'avenue.

¶

Avaler de tout clous vis à bois bouteilles d'encre
Clefs de boîtes à sardines morceaux de trente-trois tours
Pilules de nembuthal arsenic gardénal
Bretelles très souples en boule vrais faux billets de banque
Dans une isba tatare se pendre adieu assez
Avec une cravate un fil de téléphone
Une corde à sauter dans le vide une ficelle
Un lacet une ceinture un ruban de madame
Se jeter de ponts fiers corniches et tours eiffel
S'empaler sur une épée sur une broche à poulet
Se noyer en seine grise dans l'alcool la tamise
Cartonner au stand de tir avec pistolet forain
Ouvrir le four le gaz prendre une lame dans son bain
Toutes choses à nos fins arbres fleuves et puis zut!

¶

She's a stranger here she puts her earring in
A leaf is skittering the wind before her flies
Down the long avenue each he each she prepares
With colours perfumes cloth to make a splash
Or just to step outside and face the weather
Understand the world or himself herself better
Mushroom cloud the scent of jasmine a full moon
Right at the darkest end of a day of rain
The brownish trace of shit on a hollow-eyed man's jeans
Deprived for light-years of a loaf a roof a shag
Of love full stop he must have stumbled missed
A step a turning an expected crossing
When she starts to walk again the tree's so bare
Along the avenue how many trees there are.

¶

Swallow anything like nails or wood-screws ink
The keys of sardine-tins or shards of vinyl 33s
Pills of Nembutal or arsenic or phenobarbitone
Rolled-up super-stretchy braces real forged notes
In a Tartar izba hang yourself enough goodbye
From a knotted tie a spiral flex of phone
A skipping-rope to skip off in the void
A string a shoe-lace belt a ribbon of Madame's
Or throw yourself from lofty bridges ledges Eiffel tower
Stick yourself with sword or chicken-skewer
Drown yourself in alcohol the leaden Seine the Thames
Get top marks as a marksman at the fairground stall
Open the gas-tap take a bath with blades
Everything can serve our ends trees rivers what the hell.

¶

Voilà maintenant suis fixée
J'ai l'âge où un gars défoncé
Dans un métro de nuit bondé
Éructe et me tend un billet
Pas du tout doux pas doux du tout
Un billet rose pourtant mais bouh
Billet de banque de dix euros –
C'est pour t'acheter une teinture –
Je n'ai pas compris tout de suite
N'ai pas saisi du premier coup
Le message en sa vacherie
Quand je suis sortie à l'air libre
La lune éclairait sans scrupules
Les gens les choses jusqu'aux racines.

¶

À un moment on tombe dessus
Ça tombe sur nous sans un warning
Et alors on ne sait pas trop
Ce que c'est quand ce truc s'impose
D'un coup il faut porter un masque
Avaler tout un pilulier
Ça vient te sonder t'entuber
Te poser à l'horizontale
Comment allez-vous ce matin
Ça te met au poumon un drain
La vie parle de rémission
Comment vous sentez-vous ce soir
Alors là c'est qu'il se fait tard
On ferme les yeux là-dessus.

¶

I get the picture now I'm at the age
Where a young guy high as a kite
On a packed tube train at night
Belches and reaches me a note
No love note no not love no love at all
Although a pink one too but oh okay
A bank-note for ten euros –
Go and get yourself a dye –
I didn't understand at once
At first I didn't even get
The message in all its nastiness
When I came out into the free air
The moon with no such scruples lit
All things all people right down to the root.

¶

At a certain moment you trip over it
It falls on you without a gardyloo
You hardly know
Exactly what it is this whatsit that's wormed in
And all at once you have to wear a mask
And swallow down a whole small box of pills
It comes to sound you out connect you to a tube
To lay you flat
With how are you this morning
Puts a drain into your lung
And talks of life remission
How do you feel this evening
And you know that means that now it's getting late
You shut your eyes on it.

¶

pour Michèle Guigon

Mozart il fallait que j'écrive
Un mot pour tester mon crayon
Flambant nouveau allègrement
Et dire un requiem à l'autre
Crayon qui ne crayonnait plus
Et ne pouvait plus se tailler
Ne m'avançait à moi plus rien
Un petit mort dedans ma main
Mauvaise mine il ne traçait plus
Alors je lui ai mis Mozart
Le beau Requiem de Mozart
Pendant que son successeur crisse
Ces quelques traits sur le papier
Commence son exercitation.

¶

Dans la multicolore foule de la gare
Les venues les allées des autres des uns
Parmi les cheminots le monde
Je croise un beau garçon aux cheveux blancs
Sa queue de cheval est tenue par une pince
À linge verte comme du printemps doucement
Herbe aussi folle qu'elle en a l'air
Vert d'eau calme pleine de grenouilles prêtes
À crever le plafond de leur chant
La voûte mal céleste de la gare grouillante
De gens plus ou moins encombrants
Plus ou moins encombrés de gens
Allant venant dont ce garçon furtif
Pour qui j'en pince juste en passant.

¶

for Michèle Guigon

Mozart I had to write
A word to test my pencil out
This brand new allegretto writer
Say a requiem for the other
Pencil now its days of pencilling are over
It had failed to make a point
And profited myself no further
Little death inside my palm
Its leaden features could not make a mark
And so I put on Mozart for its sake
The lovely Requiem
While its successor squeaks
These scanty strokes on paper
Now its time of exercitement's come.

¶

In the multicoloured station crowd
Comings and goings of that group or this
Among the railway-workers the world's fray
I cross paths with a dishy white-haired guy
His pony-tail is held back with a peg
A spring-green clothes-peg green as gentleness
His weeds and waving grasses crazy as they seem
Green of still water full of frogs pumped up
Ready to lift the roof off with their song
The uncelestial vault of the station concourse
Crawling with people more or less in my path
My own path barred by bodies more or less
Of which this furtive guy is one I fancy
Plucking in passing in my fingertips.

93

¶

Propriétaire de rien
Employée de personne
Ma vie me l'improvise
Au fur et à mesure
Apples and pears
I go upstairs
Argot rimé ficelle
Je grimpe à mon échelle
Quand m'éprouvette grenouille
Devinette météo
Avec vieux scoubidou
M'entête et perds mes vers
C'est pépins pour ma pomme
Je coupe en deux cette poire.

¶

Le gosse claudique après son père qui marche vite
Il a un sautillement de moineau piaf meurtri
Il dit j'ai vu dans la télé s'essouffle
Pour rattraper intéresser la grande personne
Quel sera le futur de ce gamin qui penche
Petit bonhomme blessé à la patte un peu folle
Visant des yeux du front le dos du paternel
Je n'aime pas les enfants plus qu'étoiles anémones
Mais ce môme déjà presque tordu à sept ans
Qui essaie de courir après son géniteur
M'a donné l'émotion d'un frisson attardé
Porte-t-il un prénom de poisson comme Colin
Va-t-il redoubler très bientôt son CE1
Se pendre à dix-sept ans à un pont métallique.

¶

Nothing's rightful owner
No one' s employee
I improvise my life
As and when each day
Apples and pears
I mount the stairs
A string of rhyming slang
Send myself up each rung
As I forecast myself a frog
Trying to guess the weather
With an old scoobydoo
Forget my lines obsessed
My apple's got the pip
I cut this pear in two.

¶

The kid limps after his dad who's walking fast
He skip-hops like a chirping crippled sparrow
Says I saw it on the telly getting out of breath
To catch bring back the grown-up's interest
What will his future be this leaning child
This little guy with his trailing damaged foot
Eyes front and levelled at paternity's turned back
I don't love children any more than stars anemones
But this kid seven and already almost twisted up
Trying to run after his progenitor
Gave me the small shock of a delayed shudder
Does he have a fishy name like Colin
Is he about to take his first school year again
Hang himself from a metallic bridge at seventeen.

¶

Cavalière retrouvée pendue avec sa longe
Peloton de gendarmes volontaires la cherchaient
Pourtant elle était mère mariée dit le journal
Un suicide tout y laisse penser le corps sans vie
Sans la moindre trace de violences subies intact
La quadragénaire prenait des tranquillisants
Infirmière de métier elle avait disparu
En forêt une semaine quand on la découvrit
Caractère dépressif dans son blouson une lettre
Son cheval reparut au lendemain du geste
Fatal à quelques pas du centre équestre hennir
Le journal ne précise pas ce cri mais que l'arbre
Où la femme s'est assurément donné la mort
Était très en retrait et difficile d'accès.

¶

Téléphone sonne dans une poubelle
Litter litter litter litter
À London Bridge septembre s'enjambe
Quelqu'un doit parler dans le vide
Ou plutôt quelqu'un doit parler
À la machine à répondre hé
Later later later later
Le fleuve coule alors que les gens
Communiquent les gens comme uniques
Portables et jetables sommes aussi
Des fois sommes aussi tous comptes faits
Des fois que le temps crève assez
Nuageusement sur chaque banc
Amer amer bitter ailleurs.

¶

Horsewoman found hanged with leading-rein
A squad of volunteer policemen searched for her
And yet she was a mother married the paper said
A suicide it all adds up the lifeless body
Quite unmarked by outside violence intact
The forty-something was on tranquilisers
Nurse by trade when she had disappeared
When she was found she'd been in the woods a week
Prone to depression in her jacket pocket was a letter
Her horse had reappeared the morning after
A few steps from the riding stables whinnying
The paper's vague about the cry but tells us that the tree
The woman no doubt chose to kill herself
Was very inaccessible and set a long way back.

¶

Phone ringing in a waste-bin
Litter litter litter litter
London Bridge September oversteps itself
Someone must be talking in the void
Or rather someone must be talking
To the answerphone that answers hey
Later later later later
The river flows while people share
Their information in formation
Mobile and disposable as we are too
And sometimes all accounted for as well
All things considered when the cloudy weather
Bursts its cloud on every bitter bench
In *bitter* bitter bitter otherwhere.

¶

Apprivoisons la solitude sans fil
Wifi oui fi des sempiternelles prises
Électriques rallonges et tutti quanti
Dans l'arbre d'hiver un nid de pie
L'oiseau noir et blanc ses trésors
Ses vols splendides et wireless
Une alliance d'or pur au poirier
Fidèle le ciel peut témoigner
Du bleu en fond d'écran oui fi
Des cordes froides des jours de pluie
Technicien des averses envoie
De l'eau à ma petite soucoupe
Pour la magie d'un effet loupe
La petite histoire jacassée.

¶

Je vous visiterai mes amis inconnus
Au sol dans les nuages je ne vous louperai
Aussi sûr que j'aurai dans ma chaussure
Un petit gravillon pour m'agacer le pied
Une plume collée sous ma semelle aussi
Un mégot antérieur long rêve de fumée
Ou crottin de cheval herbe mal essuyée
Réminiscence douce et dormante douce
Mes amis inconnus je m'assoirai dessus
Votre seul cœur de marbre
Dur et pur comme un chêne
J'ôterai de mon soulier le caillou blanc
Et je vous chanterai une chanson mince
À l'intérieur tout noir de moi.

¶

Let's tame our loneliness without a wire
Wifi or fie on never-ending sockets plugs
Extension-leads and so forth *tutti quanti*
In the winter tree a magpie's nest
A bird in black and white its treasure-chest
The glory of its flight is wire-less
A pure gold ring circles the pear-tree's branch
The sky bears faithful witness the original
Of screens' blue wallpaper. Why fie
On the cold cords of rain that fall
On rainy days technician of the showers scatter
Water here on my small saucer
Magnify by magic as if under glass
The little story of a magpie's chatter.

¶

I'll come and visit you my unknown friends
On earth and in the clouds I won't fall wide
Of you as surely as I'll have inside my shoe
A little gravel-chip to prick my foot
A feather stuck there too beneath the sole
A former cigarette-butt long-held dream of smoke
Or horse-dung blade of unwiped grass
A sweet and dormant sweet remembering
My unknown friends I will sit down upon
Your one and only heart your marble heart
That's hard and pure as oak
I'll take my shoe off take the white stone out
And sing you a thin song
From inside my so very dark insides.

¶

Un grand juron jaillit quand je sors de ma chambre
Hôtel Victor Hugo rue des Fleurs à Dijon
La femme de ménage s'est trompée de produit
A aspergé de détartrant toute une vitre
Maintenant la fenêtre est irrécupérable
Sa voix claire m'explique l'étourderie voilà
Les flacons se ressemblent elle a voulu vite faire
Bien faire et à présent elle en a pour des heures
Il va neiger on le sent à nos pieds gelés
On le voit au carreau pulvérisé gris blanc
On l'entend dans l'air grelot maigre d'hiver
Les flocons se ressemblent aussi un peu beaucoup
Les grains de sable de sel et de poussière
Les mouches mortes idem les hommes d'affaires.

¶

Je voudrais conduire un corail jusqu'à la mer
Là m'attendrait Arlette qui m'appela Lunette
À cause des marées des affaires de phoebé
Les rails toujours une bonne échelle
De la terre sans anges mais avec des huîtres des huîtres
Qui roulent des yeux pardon pardon
La faute au vent la faute au sable
À toutes les images écoulées
Dans une poche une épître dans une poche un mouchoir
Du papier recyclé pour essayer
De crever l'abcès dent par dent
Pour ne pas essuyer ce refus ni l'eau grise
L'humeur perlière jusqu'à l'horizon
À monture d'hippocampe.

¶

When I leave my room a hefty curse rings out
In Hôtel Victor Hugo Rue des Fleurs Dijon
The cleaning woman's got the product wrong
And sprinkled with descaler this whole glass
Now the window's written off
Her lilting voice explains the daft mistake you see
The bottles look alike she had to get it done
Done well and quickly now it'll take her hours
It's threatening to snow we feel it in our frozen feet
We see it in the panes pocked grey and white
We hear it in the air thin shake of winter's bells
And snowflakes are alike as well a little bit a lot
Like grains of sand and salt and dust
And also flying businessmen dead flies.

¶

I'd like to drive a Coral train right to the sea
Where Arlette would be waiting called me her Lunette
Because of tides and moon-stuff Phoebeish affairs
Where the rails are always right their gauge the scale
To scale the sky no angels up and down
But oysters oysters roll their eyes oh pardon please excuse
It was the wind's fault or the sand's
The fault of all the images spilled out
Inside a pocket an epistle or a pocket handkerchief
Recycled paper in a grim attempt
To burst the abscess tooth by tooth
And not soak up the water of this last rejection all its grey
A pearly atmosphere as far as the horizon
While a sea-horse carries me away.

¶

Tout du long à la voie de chemin de fer
Pousse le pissenlit aux visages confiants mille
Y aurait-il un dieu jaune une joie
De fleur simplissime présente là
Personne ne s'arrête pour cueillir un bouquet
De pisse-en-lit dents-de-lion officinale taraxacum
Pourtant avec le bleu du ciel ça donne du vert
Ça se mange en salade amère se mâche
Longuement en rêvant mêmement
Kilomètres de pissenlits de ville en ville
Processions vaillantes traçant la route
Sont-elles sur la carte michelin sur le plan
Google earth en méridiens d'or pauvre
Parallèles du levant au couchant.

¶

Anniversaire jour que voilà
Tomaž Šalamun m'a griffé
Une carte postale d'Extrême-Orient
Oui le monde est encore énorme
Et c'est plus gros qu'une montagne
D'avoir un jour dix fois sept ans
Mille fois combien et des poussières
D'éternelles magies de neige neige
Énorme tout ce temps cette beauté
En partage de lumière oblique
À la fois grave et légère j'erre
La montagne flotte et s'évapore
Bleu blanc blanc bleu bleu blanc bleu bleu
Voici un jour complètement.

¶

Down the whole track-length of the railway-line
Grow the dandelions with their trustful faces
In their thousands might there be a yellow god delight
To see this flower there the simplest and the best
Though no one stops to gather up a bunch
Of piss-a-beds of lions'-teeth medicinal taraxacums
And yet with this sky's blue they give us green
You eat them in a bitter salad chewed
Unhurriedly while dreaming the same dream
Of miles of dandelions stretched from town to town
In brave procession tracing out the way
Are they marked on maps the Michelin the plan
On Google Earth meridians of poor man's gold
These parallels from farthest east to west.

¶

Birthday this fine day and look
Tomaž Šalamun has scratched me out
A postcard posted far in the far East
Yes the world's still vast
And bigger than a mountain
To be one day ten times seven
Thousand times how many specks of dust
The endless magic transformations of the snow the snow
Enormous and such beauty all that time
Our shared inheritance the angled light
That's simultaneously serious and playful now I'm wandering
The mountain floats evaporates
In blue white white blue blue white white blue white
This day's a day completely and complete.

¶

Dans son camion express et logistique
Un sandwich mayonnaise lui destine des moustaches
Il sourit pour la route et trace bien droit devant
Traversant j'imagine des villes entières en temps
Et en heure car ça tourne il faut passer vitesses
Sans écraser le petit chat ni la vieille dame
Ni le frère de sa sœur qui répare des machines
Rassemble des morceaux dans une touffeur d'usine
Manger sans perdre une seconde un casse-dalle
Écouter la radio d'une oreille avertie
Rock ou jazz météo informations loto
S'agit d'abord de gagner son logis s'agit
D'arriver sans tarder avant d'être surpris
Par la nuit qui avale hommes express logistiques.

¶

J'ai bien quatorze kilos à perdre
Si ça pouvait se faire seulement
En traçant le même nombre de lignes
Retrouver la ligne en sonnant
Je mesure l'épaisseur du temps
Ma quarantaine sans amour sauf
Ses poignées qui ne fondent pas
De foyer dont n'ai le désir
Je mange des pâtes sucres lents
Et je m'empâte sûrement
Au parmesan passent les ans
Encore deux vers et j'ai fini
Ma complainte par trop pondérale
Avec ses sept moches rimes en ã.

¶

Driving his express logistic truck
Moustache egged on by sandwich mayonnaise
He smiles just for the road and draws a line
Straight forward crosses I imagine them whole towns
Right on the clock it's turning got to shift change down
In order to avoid the kitten or the crone
His sister's brother who repairs machines
Puts bits together in the fug of factories
Not lose a single second eating a lunchtime snack
While listening to the radio with ears attuned
To rock or jazz the weather lottery the news
The only thing that counts is getting home the thing
Is getting there without a hold-up not be overtaken
By the night that swallows up express logistic men.

¶

I must lose fourteen pounds at least
If only that could happen just
By tracing the same sum of lines
Get back my figure with a rhyme
For now I measure thickened time
My fast from love my quarantine
Love-handles that will not melt down
To found a family for which I've no desire
So I eat slowly sweets and piles of pasta paste
And there's no doubt I'm piling on the weight
The years come by on camembert and brie
Just two lines more and I'll be there
And finished my too ponderous complaint
With seven *rimes insuffisantes* in -ine and -air.

¶

Parfois n'avion ni train ni bus on n'arrive pas
Depuis le matin tête de travers
Le passage est bloqué dans la glace les nuages
On ne bougera pas notre joue triste
Notre main froide notre carcasse notre habitude
On rêvera en observant le poisson rouge
Le pot de ciboulette à l'épicière
Au coin de la rue patates ragots ragoûts
On n'ira n'à l'usine n'à l'arcadie
N'aura nul cœur à balancer entre les deux
On restera sur la paille d'une vieille chaise
Demeurer fatal comme un os de seiche
Un petit oiseau jaune et très en cage
Une trompette-de-la-mort un commérage.

¶

Rester dedans à regarder dehors
Les voisins ont bouché le ciel de ma lucarne
En installant une parabole pour la télé
Mais vision de la lune c'est toujours moi qui l'ai
Je cesse de prendre des nouvelles du monde
À quoi mes petites lignes ne changent rien
D'ailleurs cette parabole dit assez long
De cela qui me navre désole
L'œil du renard coursé à travers champs
Par la petite gamine aux grosses dents
A traversé rapide ma caboche
Ou mon cœur peut-être que sais-je
De cet immense chantier très éprouvant
De nos vies ratages sentiments.

¶

Sometimes ex-planed un-trained gone bussed we don't arrive
Since morning with our heads all inside-out
There's no way out and in the mirror clouds
We won't be shifting our sad cheeks
Cold hands our carcass customary way of life
We'll dream and watch the goldfish swimming round and round
The pot-bound pot of chives bought at the grocer's store
On the street-corner spuds and scrag-end gossip stews
We won't be going either to the factory or to arcadia
Won't have the heart to leap from one to t'other
We'll stay here on the straw of an old chair
Though staying's deadly as the bones of cuttlefish
A little yellow bird and very caged
A horn of plenty stray malicious phrase.

¶

To stay in while looking out
My neighbours have blocked up my skylight's sky
By putting in a dish for their TV
Though I am still the one to have a view of moon
I've stopped receiving news of the outside world
In which my little lines can't change a thing
And anyway this dish says quite enough
Of what distresses me and brings me down
The eye of the fox hunted across the fields
By the little kid with her big teeth
Shot through my head
Or heart perhaps what do I know
Of that enormous very trying busy-ness
Of how we live our failures feelings mess.

¶

Encore un train bondé de culs de militaires
En toile de camouflage la même pour leurs gros sacs
Pas de quoi se tourner impossible d'atteindre
Les vécés le wagon-bar en voiture quatre
Les culs les innombrables derches du vendredi
Aux heures de pointe d'enfer complet
Fonce le tégévé investi par l'armée
Bidasses en permission de couleur caca d'oie
Ça vous donne la nausée ces verdâtres mélangés
De mauvais goût chierie panoplie poulailler
Treillis pour les soldats c'est solide et grossier
Une petite valise bleue a sombré sous le poids
Des bagages kakis noirs énormes bouchant la vue
Imprenable des paysages d'évasion belle.

¶

Il y a un gros vase noir vide rempli d'eau de pluie qui attend
Une petite voiture blême pour les fleurs finies ou cassées
Si je me perds avec mon paquet d'anémones mon tas de papiers
Mon amas de moi mal amarré
Les cimetières sont des lieux carrés et quadrillés
Un peu comme la feuille où je trace ces lignes
Rien d'aussi beau qu'une main d'arbre nervures d'érable
De peuplier de charme d'orme
Mains d'automne mortes et vive le vent
Il m'a fallu tout mercredi pour ne pas revenir de mardi
M'admettre et démettre en pensement avec vous être
Encore avec vous être encore avec vous être encore
Quelque part n'importe où avec vous n'être
Un gros vase noir vide rempli d'eau de pluie qui m'entend.

¶

Another train packed out with soldiers' arses
Dressed in camouflage the same as their fat bags
You can't turn round impossible to reach
The loo the buffet-bar in carriage four
The Friday arses bums without a number
Every rush-hour it's a hell on wheels
It hurtles this express cut off and cordoned by the army
Squaddies all on leave the shade of goose-crap
Makes you nauseous this mixture of off-green
Bad taste and shit the palette of a hen-coop
Battledress for soldiers solid crude
A small blue case has sunk beneath the weight
Of bags in khaki black enormous blocking out the view
That can't be seen of open country great escape.

¶

There's a big black empty vase of rainwater whch waits
A small pale cart for dead or broken-headed flowers
In case I should get lost my parcel of anemones my pile of papers
Hank of hankerings this badly-anchored me
A cemetery's a place ruled out in squares
A little like the sheet of paper where I write these lines
Nothing as lovely as the hands of trees the nerves of maples
Poplars hornbeams elms
Dead hands of autumn and long live the wind
It took me all of Wednesday not to get over Tuesday
Admit it to myself dismiss all soothing thought of how to be with you
Again with you to be with you again still be
Somewhere anywhere with you not be
A big black empty vase of rainwater which hears.

¶

Arbre arbre plutôt que marbre
Quand j'aurai fini terminé
Alors je n'aurai pas pour rien
Usé tant de papier
Faites-moi un lopin agnostique
Une petite partie de jardin
Et surtout ne gravez que dalle
Comme le temps passe le souvenir
Reste même si la formule
Ne manque pas de profondeur
Plantez un chêne pour la rouzeau
Du vertical pour l'horizon
Puis de l'herbe bien folle autour
Plutôt qu'un gazon dormitif.

¶

Mon avion est délayé
I mean my plane is delayed
Moi qui voulais rester ici
Dans la très profonde Angleterre
Il a neigé à Heptonstall
Et sur ma tête simultanée
My plane is delayed soit j'attends
Café sandwich œuf mayonnaise
J'attends et je ne rien comprends
Aux paroles de l'aéroport
Je ne rien entends il tombe tant
De flocons tout blancs en même temps
Mon avion retardé bientôt
Noël je m'arrive à l'oreille.

¶

A tree a growing tree and not a stone
When I have finished when I'm done
So I won't have used in vain
Used up worn out so many sheets of paper
Make me a small agnostic patch of ground
A little scrap of garden
Above all don't engrave a thing
Like time goes by yet memories
Remain no matter if the ready-cut-out phrase
Is deep enough
So plant an oak for me for la Rouzeau
A something vertical for the horizon
Weeds and grasses round it in a crazy straggle
Rather than a soporific lawn.

¶

My plane has been diluted
Je veux dire my plane's delayed
And wasn't I just wishing I could stay
Here in deepest England
Over Heptonstall it's snowed
And on my simultaneous head
My plane's retarded so okay I'll wait
Coffee a sandwich egg mayo
I wait I nothing understand
Of airportspeak
I nothing hear so many falling flakes
so whitely simultaneous and here
My plane's *délayé* Christmas coming soon
and I'm arriving up to my own ear.

¶

Pour peu que j'entende bien quoi
Que ce soit à quoi que ce soit
Tout à l'heure me croyais demain
Je m'étais endormie en plein dans tout à l'heure
Puis dans très simplement le même jour au réveil
En mille ici à vivre présentement
Parmi les gens les animaux les plantes
Qui savent donner la date exacte
Les jours c'est là où nous vivons
Je répète le poète encore
Avec ou sans calendrier
Ce vieux dimanche lent de novembre
Je m'étire longuement je vois
Un ciel tomber sur mes carreaux.

¶

Encore un camion votre fuel sur un coup de fil
Je remonte fichu fil impossible
Disparu pareil que l'élégant ptérodactyle
Mais je n'ai pas besoin de fioul
Par contre ma mère si ta merci
Et tant de monde à vivre en même temps
Sans merci de wireless fidelity
Un ange a du mal à passer
Fil conducteur salut chauffeur
Universel routier ave mes frères
Frères de sang frères de chant frères de vent
Adoncques voilà un coup sans fil
J'entends les paroles s'emmêler
Avec les vitesses à passer.

¶

Not far from really understanding
Nothing of anything
Just now I thought we were tomorrow
Dozed off in the midst of later on
Then woke up simply to a day that hadn't changed
These days I chase my tail
Living among people animals and plants
Who have no trouble pinning a date down
Days are where we live
I say the poet's words again
With or without a calendar
This slow old Sunday in November
Take time out to stretch and see
A falling sky that spills across my panes.

¶

Another truck with fill up on your phone
I try to find the broken line again impossible
It's flown off elegantly as a pterodactyl
I don't need to be filled up with fuel
My mum on the other hand and mercy yours
So many people in a life at once
No thanks no mercy from 'wireless fidelity'
An angel hardly has the space to pass
Along the wire transmitting to the driver
Hi the universal greeting of the roads I greet you brothers
My blood brothers my sang brothers brothers of the wind
And thus this call without the help of wires
I hear our words entwine
Accompanied by changes through the gears.

¶

Le temps ne passait plus ni la blanquette de veau
Lorsque mon père a quitté des vaches le plancher
Papa comme une plume oui mon père si léger
Qu'est-ce qu'il aurait duré papa dans cet état
Aérien d'homme en train d'être un ange tout petit
Mon papa diminuait avec mon espérance
Quand même il était aussi jaune qu'un poisson clown
Au mois de février de quatre-vingt-dix-sept
Au cœur d'avant-printemps il ne respira plus
Les fourmis allaient travailler sans lui toujours
Les belles oies voleraient sans lui pareil la lune
La lune fabriquerait des ronds et des croissants
À jamais le gros monde ferait sans papa plume.

¶

On me demande de rédiger une note de frais
Et moi je pense au fond de l'air
Je sonde ma personne facture donc
Ma crève et mon temps de parole
Tant de paroles pour une intro
Vertie comme moi il faut tenir
Vertie convertie à mourir
De trac de trouille tracasserie
À sonner mots justes et injustes
Palabres graves ou devinettes
Sornettes voire onomatopées
Le palpitant au maximum
Du nombre de ses coups minute
Boum j'ai écrit et j'ai signé ma note de frais.

¶

When my father shuffled off this mortal coil
Time would not be stomached like that casserole
And dad a feather then my father was so light
Oh how he could have lasted daddy in that state
Of airiness a man becoming angel and so small
My father shrinking with the hope I'd feel
And even though he was as yellow as a clown-fish
In the month of February ninety-seven at the heart
Of just-before-the-spring when he stopped breathing
Ants still ran about and worked without him
Geese would fly without him just the same the moon
The moon would make its circles and its crescents
The big world without a feather daddy would go on.

¶

I'm asked to put down my expenses in a note
And here's me thinking in the highest air
I plumb my depths so yes an invoice here
My own exhaustion my time on parole
So many voiced *paroles* for an intro
Vert like me you must hold on
Avert converted as you are to death
By heart-stop stage-fright harassment
To sound out the *mot juste* the word unjust
The grave confabulations riddles still unguessed
Or onomatopoeias balderdash to boot
To crank up palpitation to the max
Of numbered beats per minute
Boom I've written signed my invoice note.

¶

À la maîtresse offrent des noix
De l'amour-en-cage lumineux
Bouquet de fin d'automne un feu
Pour son logis très assombri
Après la classe longtemps la hantent
Les écoliers leurs voix perchées
Poésies au pas cadencé
Ah oui s'enfuir oui s'envoler
Aller voir ailleurs dégager
Ficher le camp loin des casernes
Des pédagogiques entreprises
Remplacer les scolaires bulletins
Par surprise météo qu'on vote
La neige la plus grande vacance.

¶

pour Susan Wicks

Au BHV grand Bazar de l'Hôtel de Ville
De Paris et non pas Grand Bazar d'Istanbul
Rayon vaisselle devant la porcelaine anglaise
Je me suis voyagée soudain à Sissinghurst
Tout en haut de la tour de Vita Sackville-West
J'avais essayé le chapeau d'une fleur énorme
De camélia d'albâtre plus grosse que toute ma tête
Au jardin de l'amie de Virginia Byzance
Avec Sue et le blanc le bleu du végétal
Le thé délice l'après-midi puis vers le soir
Une sensation de fantôme en promenade
Maintenant je rentrais avec mon souvenir
Rue Brisemiche rue de la Verrerie rue du Renard
De soucoupes de bouquets partagés.

¶

They bring their teacher hearts
In cages chinese lanterns luminous
Bouquet for end of autumn or a fire
To light her darkened rooms
After the class for days the children haunt
Her with their high-pitched voices
Poems that hop and skip
Ah yes to run away yes fly
To see what gives elsewhere clear out
Clear off far from the military barracks
Pedagogical providers and endeavours
Swap these regular reports from school
For a weather-check surprise in which you vote
For snow the greatest vacancy of all.

¶

for Susan Wicks

At the big Bazar de l'Hôtel de Ville the BHV
In Paris not the Grand Bazaar in Istanbul
The crockery department by the English china
I was suddenly transported back to Sissinghurst
The tower-top of Vita Sackville-West
I'd tried on an enormous flower like a hat
Camellia of alabaster bigger than my head
In Virginia's friend's garden a Byzantium
With Sue and then the white one the leaf-blue
And tea that afternoon delicious then as evening fell
The feeling of a ghost let out to take a stroll
And now as I came back I brought this memory
Along the rue Brisemiche rue de la Verrerie rue du Renard
Of saucers and bouquets of flowers shared.

¶

Sa petite tête dans la grosse cuillère
Dehors loin ne casse pas les vitres
N'appelle pas à jouer au ballon
Au terrain vague à l'aventure des pieds
À la tête il se voit dans la cuillère à soupe
Avec un effet loupe et déformant marrant
Même s'il rame beaucoup en ce bol tiédasse
Des yeux gras flottent à la surface pouah
On dirait des regards morts exorbités
De poissons d'argent aux silences d'or
Fixant le plafond pourri la bouche d'enfant
Tordue dans la cuillère énormément ment ment
Qui ne dit rien pleine de sa solitude
Son anguille d'avaler de travers.

¶

Quelque chose de joyeux en ce garçon pédale
Plus vite que le tramway plus vite que ma pensée
Toute la longue avenue de Flandre aux arbres nus
En danseuse sur le trottoir parallèle
Aux rails ce garçon grimpe avec gaîté
On dirait depuis ma fenêtre au Nord
D'où je songe alors au maillot à pois
Beau Tour de France depuis mille neuf cent trois
On se moque d'être meilleur ou pas meilleur
Quand le désir nous roule ailleurs ailleurs
Les roues cyclistes rayonnent tantôt soleils
Et tantôt lunes d'argent lunes allumées
D'aluminium au rêve léger grâce à
Gracieuse belle dynamique bonne dynamo.

¶

His little head reflected in the great big spoon
Outside's a long way off it doesn't break a pane
Or call on him to go out and play ball
On a bit of waste-land an adventure for his feet
As for his head he sees himself in the soup-spoon's bowl
Distorted magnified it makes him laugh
Even if he's struggling in the luke-warm bath
With eyes of grease that float on the surface yuk
You'd think they were the bulging stone-dead eyes
Of silver fish with golden silences
Staring at the rotten ceiling the childish mouth
Twisted inside a giant soup-spoon where it lies
Lies lies the mouth which full of loneliness is mute
And full of eel that's gone down the wrong way.

¶

Something joyful in this boy is pedalling
Faster than the tramcar faster than my thoughts
Along the avenue de Flandre with its bare trees
Up on the pedals like a dancer all along the path
That parallels the tramlines he's light-hearted as he climbs
As far as I can see him from my window in the Nord
Where I'm dreaming now of spotted jerseys
Glorious Tour de France first run nineteen-oh-three
Who cares about the better or not better
When desire is speeding us elsewhere
The wheels of cyclists shining now like suns
Now silver moons illuminated moons
Of aluminium with its dream of lightness by the grace
Of graceful beautiful dynamics dynamo that turns.

¶

Aussi je est un hôte d'on ne sait qui ni quoi
Mystère en bout de course comme à la balançoire
La vie assujettit drôlement ses invités
Alors je vante le vent par ma lucarne ouverte
Et je ne confonds pas auspices avec hospices
Rouzeau avec réseau dentiste avec temps triste
Pater avec par terre pleure avec meurs meurs meurs
Tu pisseras moins moins moins
Mon poème ne compte pas davantage
Que la conversation bruyante de mon prochain
M'empêchant de poursuivre par ici sauf
À fermer ma lucarne ou la repeindre en bleu
Appeler ma prochaine
Ou m'écrier au feu.

¶

Le garçon rend la mangue trop chère à la caissière
Pas assez dans son porte-monnaie pas moyen là
Pas assez transpiré pas assez de liquide
D'euros d'heures au boulot pas touché le gros lot
Il a l'œil noir le sourcil inquiété
La peau cuivrée d'aimer bien le soleil
La mangue pèse pour la peine soudain la mangue
Sur la petite balance aux fruits et aux légumes
La mangue sent le Pérou le Brésil et encore
L'oléorésine jaune ou brune térébenthine
La meilleure est celle du Mali qu'on ne trouve pas
En France où le garçon travaille et maintenant
Rien il repart voilà comme il était venu
Avec trop peu d'espèces pas de quoi.

¶

So I's the host of who knows who or what
It's like a swing a mystery as you arrive
Life rules its house-guests in the oddest ways
And so I boast about my skylight open to the breeze
And don't confuse an auspice with a hospice
Or my name with numb a sore tooth with toothed saw
Father with farther cry with die die die
You'll piss out less less less
The value of my poem won't be higher
Than my neighbour's noisy conversation
Which prevents me going on in here unless
I keep my skylight shut repaint it blue
Or call my nearest friend
Or shout Fire! Fire!

¶

The boy gives back the mango at the till too dear
He hasn't got enough to pay for it no way
He didn't sweat enough his cash-flow has run dry
His euros hours of work are not enough he hasn't won
The jackpot yet his eyes are black his eyebrows frown
With worry skin like bronze from relishing the sun
The mango's suddenly the weight of all his pains
On the little scales for fruit and vegetables
And it still smells of mango from Peru Brazil
That oily yellow resin and brown turpentine
The best ones come from Mali which you never find
In France where this boy works and now
Nothing he leaves that's it the way he came
No wherewithal you're welcome insufficient coin.

¶

Longuement espérant le tram je ruminais
Tout m'assaillait la prose journalistique le vent
Quelques proverbes comme la vérité sort toujours
De la bouche des enfants qu'un écolier lança
Le matin même très fier et sûr de lui bêta
Il avait projeté bien fort ce bête dicton
Cette noquerie d'adulte mâchonnée puis jetée
Dans l'air lourd de la classe je décollai de là
De passage je passai joyeusement les bornes
Pour sortir et songer un peu à notre vie
Sur un banc au bord du chemin de fer
Épuisant un chewing-gum à la forte menthe forte
L'envoyai d'une pichenette rouler dessus le quai
Ressemblait tout craché à cervelle miniature.

¶

Éclat de grosse perruche comme de cracher
Une graine de tournesol en poussant
Non pas une fleur mais un cri vni
Grincement de porte petit chat gonds mal huilés
Klaxon de vélomoteur de mobylette rouillée
Ça crève tympans et couche d'ozone
D'eau jaune affreux affreux strident
Ou grêle grelot chagrin avec du tremblement
Dans la voix nourrissonne six mois cent jours
Gargarismes agagax façon bébé bandit
Il y a aussi houhou variante oiseau de nuit
Petits d'homme émettent drôles de sons
D'étranges bruits décibels et s'ils pleurent
N'en pissent pas moins composent
Avec la vie la mort d'attaque déjà.

¶

I was ruminating in no hurry as I waited hoping for the tram
And it all came crowding in the journalistic prose the wind
Some proverbs like truth will out and they will out
Of the mouths of children small boy's proud retort
That very morning idiotic so sure of himself
He'd raised his voice to make the stupid saw project
That piece of adult bullshit masticated and spat out
In the heavy classroom air and I took off
In my migration overstepped the bounds with a light heart
To come outside and think a bit about our life
Here on a bench beside the tramway-line
While chewing all the flavour from a piece of gum
Strong mint ferocious flicked between my finger and my thumb
Across the platform, spitting image of a little brain.

¶

A great fat budgie-squawk as if on spitting up
A sunflower seed as it sends out
No flower but a cry that's flying unidentified
A squeaking door a kitten hinges that need oil
A motorcycle horn or moped stiff with rust
Shattering our eardrums and the ozone layer
With a yucky yucky sherbet-yellow liquid
To the tinny ring of tears with tremolo
In nursing-infant voice six months a hundred days
A gargle Agagax in baby bandit style
Or variant whoo-whoo night bird
The human young emit the weirdest sounds
The oddest noises decibels yet even as they cry
They still pee on regardless compromise
With life with death already on their toes.

¶

Quand je remplissais de cannettes le frigo
À Saint-Trop dans le Var du Croissant Chaud
Et servais aux touristes affamés des chouettes burgers
Au ketchup ou à la moutarde à la moutarde ou au ketchup
Là encore et même davantage j'étais nouvelle
Aujourd'hui je penserais aux couleurs du phoenix
Rouge et jaune ketchup moutarde jaune et rouge
Je lancerais aux mouettes les brioches périmées
Les brioches endurcies qu'il fallait attendrir
D'un coup de four à micro-ondes ou les payer
Cependant qu'à Toulon le big boss oubliait
Mes heures supplémentaires j'aurais dû les rêver
Au bord du bleu de la belle Méditerranée
Mais je l'ai dit je débutais dans l'active existence
Pas une vie et je n'étais pas libre – patate.

¶

Dans les transports en commun communs
Toujours il y a quelqu'une quelqu'un
Pour s'asseoir sur un pan un pan
Un pan de ton manteau flottant
Comme un bout d'aile ou quoi qui sort
Dépasse déborde morceau d'habit
Où un voyageur pose une fesse
Distraitement dans le trajet bref
En tramway entre Lille et Roubaix
En métro de Montrouge à Paris
Quelqu'un te retient par un rien de paletot
On se trouve quand même un rien serré
Et cahoté par la chaleur humaine.

¶

When I'd fill up the fridge with cans of drink
At Saint-Trop in the Var the Hot Croissant
And serve the famished tourists these great burgers
With a squirt of ketchup mustard mustard ketchup
There again especially then I was a new recruit
Now I'd think about the colours of the phoenix
Red and yellow ketchup mustard mustard yellow red
I'd throw the crumbs of past-their-sell-by-date brioches
To the gulls the hard brioches that I had to soften up
With a burst of microwave or pay for them myself
While in Toulon the big boss could forget
My hours of overtime I should have dreamed away
Beside the deep blue glitter of the Med
But as I said my insight into 'active life' was short
It wasn't life and I was never acting freely – just a clot.

¶

On public transport that transports us most
There's always someone someone who will sit
Sit down upon a bit a little bit
A bit of your escaping coat
That's like a wingtip or the tip of what
Which sticks out or flops over bit of cloth
Another traveller can rest his arse's cheek
On absent-mindedly the little while it takes
To cross by tram from Lille into Roubaix
By underground to Paris from Montrouge
Someone will hold you back by your coat's thread
Yet all the same you're feeling lightly squeezed
And jiggled by the warmth of human knees.

125

¶

Je n'écris pas jour d'hui
Vis dans l'éphéméride
Juste ça laisser le temps
Me passer à travers
Days are where we live
Dit le poète les jours
Sont là où nous vivons
Nous éternisons patientons
Le temps vole et fait mes rides
Il se répète autant que moi
Je rigole et montre patte d'oie
Dérape aïe c'était du verglas
Ce jeudi désespérément
Là yes mon cher Philip Larkin.

¶

Ce vingt mars d'équinoxe et rien
Un merle en haut d'un beffroi certes
Mais ma main glacée ma main verte
Ma caboche givrée gourde pensée
Équinoxe combientième déjà
Et les solstices saisons plus nettes
En chaud et froid quelques douzaines
Tant d'éphémérides effeuillées
Quel détective malin dira
Vous avez eu assez d'hivers
En deux mille cinquante cinq mettons
Ça fera deux fois quarante-quatre
Ans de soleils gelées rosées
Saisons déchaînons les saisons.

¶

Won't write a word today
I'll live the turning page
Just that to let time pass
Right through me
Days are where we live
The poet says *les jours*
Sont là où nous vivons
Where we forever wait
Time flies repetitive
As me in turn I age
I show my crow's-feet off and laugh
It's slippery oh god that was black ice
This Thursday in despair
Dear Philip Larkin yes I'm also there.

¶

The twentieth of March the equinox and nothing gives
A blackbird perched up there on a belfry true
But my frozen hand my fingers that are green
My ice-bound head the sluggish way I think
My whatieth equinox must it be now
And solstices their seasons more distinct-
Ly hot and cold six dozen or four score
So many calendars have lost their leaves
What clever-dick detective will maintain
You've had enough of winters
Say in twenty fifty-five
To make twice forty-four
Whole years of suns frosts dews
Of seasons seasons let's undo their chains.

¶

Non je ne reviens pas vers vous je viens c'est tout
Je ne vous dirai rien autour d'un verre à pied
Ne suis pas très causante encore moins conviviale
Quand vos paroles sont tellement toujours les mêmes
Interchangeables et creuses formules des tics en toc
Vive les chiens éperdus les chats égratignés
Les âmes errantes les fantômes distingués
Le sourire à l'envers de la lune dans ma tasse
J'ai l'amour spontané de mon prochain sauf quand
Mon prochain s'intéresse de trop près à mon goût
À ma personne gentille et froide et solitaire
Alors là je m'éloigne à grandes enjambées
Du buffet dînatoire où j'étais conviée
Et je rentre chez moi savourer mon congé.

¶

Asters astérisques en quoi vais-je recycler
Ma personne pas en vélo de course en grande ni petite ourse
Peut-être en réverbère ponctuel indifférent
En grenouille verte ou rousse aux mares étangs échelles
Diseuse de météo sans paroles joueuse muette
De flûte à bec avec canards vivants
Hôtesse de l'air sur terre les avions décollés
Pareillement qu'oreilles sensibles de faunes
Comment bien me convertir à deux fois
Vingt-deux ans et des poussières d'étoiles
Il faut faire quelque chose avant la fin prédite
Du monde où sommes fragiles plus que fleurs à couper
Le brouillard au couteau le tas de cartes le chat
Mistigri à travers champs il s'évapore.

¶

No I'm not back with all of you I've come that's all
I won't say anything to you around a tall-stemmed glass
I'm not too chatty much less life and soul
When all your words are always old and stale
And interchangeable just rubbish phrases box of tics
Long live the witlost dogs the scarred doneover cats
The wandering souls the grave distinguished ghosts
The moon that's smiling upturned in my cup
I can love my neighbour with impulsive love
Until my neighbour probes too closely in my tastes
My person which is kind and cold and solitary
Then I run away as fast as legs can scurry
From the buffet dinner where I was a guessed
And come back home to taste escape the best.

¶

Asters or asterisks as what shall I recycle
Me not a racing bike a great or little she-bear trike
Perhaps a street-light punctual indifferent
A frog that's green or reddish in the pond weir dike
A wordless weather-girl a silent player
Of the penny-whistle followed by a sty of china pigs
A grounded air-ghostess when all the planes have left
As lightly as the lifting ears of fauns
How can I convert myself at twice
Those two-and-twenty years and stardust
Something must be done before the warned-of end
Of the world where we are flimsier than flowers to be cut
The fog with a knife the stack of cards the cat
Called Mistigri across the fields where he evaporates.

¶

Tous les jours je traverse de parfaits inconnus
Une dame au petit chien qui boit sauvignon sec
Un gars dans un t-shirt jaune d'or pour m'éblouir
Une infirmière aux yeux froissés ma tante
Des hordes d'écoliers des centaines des myriades
Parfois certains me donnent le bourdon
Je pense au futur d'avance misérable
Un autre gars qui passe en sifflant longuement
Comme d'un baiser j'ai peur d'une abeille
C'est trop éprouvant de voir tant de prochains
Même à bonne distance bien salutaire
Inconnus les aptères bipèdes qui viennent et vont
Tous ces prochains passés je ne veux pas y aller
Comme ça toute seule à yep sans dictionnaire.

¶

Avant de descendre assurez-vous
De ne rien t'oublier
Un agréable voyage une bonne journée
Nous vous prions
De bien vouloir nous excuser
Pour la chaîne occasionnée
Votre chef d'abord
Personnel au bout du quai
Étiqueté qui t'es quitté
Abandonné suspect
Bien vouloir nous signaler
Tout objet qui paraîtrait
Nous vous remercions
De votre incompréhension.

¶

Each day these perfect strangers cross my path
A lady with a dog that drinks dry sauvignon
A guy who dazzles me with his gold T-shirt on
A nurse with night-shift-crumpled eyes my aunt
And school-kids in their hundreds in a throng
Sometimes I can't take it they can all b off
I see their lives already come to grief
Another guy who passes whistling a slow song
Like kisses I confess I have a fear of stings
Too wearing seeing all these people who are close
Even when a proper healthy distance wings
Them into air then unknown apteral bipeds come and go
And all the close ones who have passed I won't go there
Totally alone like that on foot without a *dictionnaire.*

¶

Before you leave the train make sure
You haven't left yourself or anything behind
A pleasant journey voyage a nice day
We beg you
Please excuse us
Any inconvenient ink heard
Your high reguarded guard
The staff at the platform's head
You're ticketed *id est* ticked off
A suspect abandoned person
Please bring to our attention
Any object that might seem
We thank you
For your wonderstanding.

NOTES

p. 17: 'Eden, Two, Three and Churned-up Me':
'Eden' is the Czech word for 'one'. *(vr)* The whole *Quand Je Me Deux* collection makes playful reference to the sequence of numbers from one to forty-one in its contents pages, and a number of the poems have punning numerical titles – a nod to the fact that Valérie worked on them at her kitchen 'counter'. Where it was possible in English, I've sometimes made the same kind of numerical gesture. *(sw)*

Like much of Rouzeau's work, the text of both collections is rich in nods to other poets and writers, past and present, and while I've reproduced Valérie's own notes to individual poems and added a few of my own, it hasn't been possible to flag up every one. In this poem, they include nods to St. Exupéry's *Le petit prince*, and to Ronsard's 'Mignonne, allons voir si la rose...' (IV, ll. 2-3). *(sw)*

p. 21: 'The cupboard's bare...'
This poem is particularly rich in literary reference – among the poets evoked are Rimbaud (l. 5), Desnos (ll. 12-13), Plath (l. 26) and Ginsberg (last line). *(sw)*

l. 18: 'RER': The 'Réseau Express Régional' is the Paris regional rapid transit system. *(sw)*

l. 20: 'Lu biscuits': 'Lu' stands for 'Lefèvre Utile', a manufacturer of French biscuits associated with the town of Nantes. *(sw)*

p. 33: 'Our friendship in driving rain...'
I've substituted a nod to Shakespeare for the playful nod to Mallarmé in l. 5 of the original – swelling the number of Shakespeare references already present in Valérie's text. *(sw)*

l. 6: 'ladies on the mountaintop': A reference to Apollinaire's 'Le mai le joli mai...' in *Alcools (vr)*

l. 10: 'the bird sings... at the foot of the happy man' is a reference to Tardieu's *La première personne du singulier. (vr)*

p. 35: 'Tenuous'
The title is an echo of the playful numerical references in the original contents pages. *(sw)*

p. 43: '01 43 15 50 67':
The verb tenses themselves are part of the wordplay in the French original. *(sw)*

p. 45: 'Carpe Diem':
The reference is to a poem of mine called 'Buying Fish' in *Open Diagnosis*, reprinted in *Night Toad*. *(sw)*

p. 49: 'Vain Poem':
ll. 23-25: 'wouldn't he Guillaume...?' – a reference to Apollinaire's famous characterisation of the Eiffel Tower as a shepherdess guarding her flock of bleating bridges in 'Zone'. *(sw)*

p. 51: 'The Poem for Jacques':
l. 31: 'Zaoummm': 'Zaoum' is a reference to Russian Formalist poetry, a movement dating from 1913. Za-oum means 'beyond mind', and its emphasis was on sound rather than on explicit meaning. I have added a couple of m's in English to convey the zing of the arrow. *(sw)*

p. 53: 'Objection: a love pome pour deux voix':
'Pome' in the original is a James Joyce reference *(sw)*

p. 59: 'Thirty-two Teeth':
l. 8: 'of hairs, yes yes affairs': the pun has been changed here with Valérie's blessing. *(sw)*
l. 17: No way to get the oxymoron of 'mords la vie' in English... *(sw)*

p. 61: 'Cross My Heart':
l. 8: There's a macaronic (French / English) pun here in the original. *(sw)*

p. 63: 'Gue Digue Don':
Title: 'Gue Digue Don' (etc) is a traditional folk refrain, a bit like 'Tra-la' or 'Hey nonny no'. I chose not to translate it, in this very Parisian poem. *(sw)*
p. 65, section 6, l. 2 : 'your cart of ducks and penguins': a nod to Robert Desnos' *'fourmi de dix-huit mètres'* in *Chantefables et*

Chantefleurs (vr)

p. 67, section 7, l. 3: 'We all come down from Advent and Ever After': the wordplay here in the original is on Adam and Eve and 'Ed', a chain of small French supermarkets. *(sw)*

p. 67, section 8, l. 1: 'ox and Mass': in the original French the pun is on 'âme' (soul) and the expected 'âne' (ass). Valérie herself has used the word 'Messe' in a similarly playful context in 'Le Poème pour Jacques' on p. 50.

p. 67, section 8, l. 9: 'his tin his begging bowl his muff [...]': a nod to the tin / muff in Charlie Chaplin's *A Dog's Life* (vr) The nod to Rosetti is mine. *(sw)*

p. 67, Section 9, l. 4: 'Gaston': Gaston Miron and his 'Walk to love' in the book *L'Homme rapaillé. (vr)*

p. 69: 'And I was wondering what bird...':
l. 15: 'a marvellous cloud': a reference to Baudelaire's *Petits Poèmes en prose. (sw)*

NOTES TO PART TWO: POEMS FROM 'VROUZ'

The 58 sonnets I've translated are taken from a sequence of 161 *(sw)*.

p. 73: title:
'The good word *'Vrouz'* was coined by Jacques Bonnaffé. Together with Sardine Robinson and Adèle Cockrobin, we thank him warmly – it certainly vrouzes a bit better on the ear than 'crazy self-portraits with or without self'. *(vr)*

p. 75: 'I'm good for this or nothing':
echoing Beckett's famous response for the journal *Libération*, 'all I'm good for', to the question, 'why do you write?'. *(vr)*

p. 79: 'I dreamed I lied about my bust-size':
'Dupont Dupond': The Dupont Duponds have been lightheartedly borrowed from Hergé. *(vr)* The French expression *'bonnet blanc blanc bonnet'* means 'it amounts to the same thing' in English (Collins Robert). As well as meaning 'bonnet', *'bonnet'* also refers to bra cup-size. *(sw)*

p. 81: 'Us eaters of potaters':
The poem was inspired by Van Gogh's painting, 'The Potato-eaters'. *(sw)* Four words [in the original French] have been borrowed from an old advertisement for M... mashed potato: *'petit volcan'* and *'jus dedans'*. *(vr)*

p. 83: 'To meet your soulmate...':
[The French words] *'rencontrez l'âme soeur'* [are taken from] Internet advertising. *(vr)*

p. 83: 'Today sixteenth of June...':
Bloom: reference to James Joyce's *Ulysses*, in which the epic arc describes a day in the life of a Dubliner, Leopold Bloom, 16th June 1904 (Bloomsday). Ted Hughes and Sylvia Plath had chosen that very special date as their wedding-day. *(vr)*

p. 85: 'My artificial memory? I couldn't give a toss...':
The four lines [of the original] ending in *'étoile'* ('star') are by the gracious poet Éric Sautou. *(vr)*

p. 85: 'The fingers of young mothers...':
The lexical source of this sonnet [was] the informational material, revised in 2008, for Mitosyl ointment. *(vr)*

p. 87: 'I measured my length in snow...':
'Fins vins' instead of *'vins fins'*: because [in English in the original note] the Café Rouge in question may be found in Manchester, UK. *(vr)*

p. 87: 'Negative I don't know how to take a photo no...':
'vrouz': see note to book title, above. *(sw)*

p. 89: 'Swallow anything like nails...':
Reading Rumi's very instructive work, *Suicides* (Serg, Paris, 1964) gave me a plethora of information for this poem, where the end, *'et puis zut!'* is from Jacques Rigaut, a whimsical poet who swore he would kill himself on the day of his thirtieth birthday, 5 November 1929, and was faithful to his undertaking. The sonnet also evokes in particular the respective suicides of

Marilyn Monroe (l. 3); Marina Tsvetaeva (l. 5); Gérard de Nerval (l. 8, the 'ribbon of madame's' being, according to legend, Madame de Maintenon's); Paul Celan, Sylvia Plath (l. 13). *(vr)*

p. 93: 'Mozart I had to write…':
The word at the end is from Montaigne, who gave the title 'on Exercitation' to the sixth chapter of the second book of his *Essays*, it could be translated as 'experience'. *(vr)* But here the archaic word rings almost like a coinage, and surely means something more…? *(sw)*

p. 95: 'Nothing's rightful owner…':
l. 9: 'forecast myself a frog': the reference is apparently to the weather-predicting properties of frogs. *(sw)*

p. 97: 'Horsewoman found hanged with leading-rein…':
[The words] *'Pourtant elle était mère'*; *'Sans la moindre trace de violences subies'*; *'Caractère dépressif'*; *'très en retrait et difficile d'accès'* [in the original]: printed in *Métro Paris*, Monday 10 January 2011. *(vr)*

p. 99: 'I'll come and visit you my unknown friends…':
'My unknown friends' are also a bit like those of Jules Supervielle. *(vr)*

p. 101: 'I'd like to drive a Coral train…':
l. 6 'oysters roll their eyes': a nod to Robert Desnos, whose partner, Youki, used to say that he had magnificent oyster eyes. *(vr & sw)*

p. 103: 'Down the whole track-length of the railway-line…':
'The first dandelion shows its trustful face', says Walt Whitman in his *Blades of Grass*… *(vr)*

p. 103: 'Birthday this fine day and look…':
'The world is still enormous.' A quote from Tomaž Šalamun on the back of a postcard from China. *(vr)*

p. 105: 'Driving his express logistic truck…':

ll. 13-14: *'Surpris par la nuit'* [in the original]: the title of one of Alain Veinstein's programmes on *France Culture* [radio]. *(vr)*

p. 105: 'I must lose fourteen pounds at least...':
The translation of this poem and our resulting dialogue showed me very clearly that for Valérie the number fourteen, with its sonnet association, was far more important than the actual value of a pound or a kilogram! I've also taken liberties with the cheeses, and with the punning French insertion in the last line, which Valérie has endorsed. *(sw)*

p. 107: 'Sometimes ex-planed un-trained...':
I have a feeling *'fatal comme un os de seiche'* [in the original] might be from Christian Bachelin... *(vr)*

p. 111: 'A tree a growing tree...':
l. 11: *'la Rouzeau'*: echoes here of La Fontaine's *'Le Chêne et le roseau'*, and perhaps too of Pascal's 'roseau pensant'... *(vr & sw)*

p. 111: 'My plane has been diluted...':
the French word *'délayé'* means 'diluted'. *(sw)*

p. 113: 'Not far from really understanding...': '
Days are where we live' is a line by the poet Philip Larkin. *(vr)*

p. 113: 'Another truck with fill up on your phone...':
The words *'Votre fuel sur un coup de fil'* were written in large letters on the truck. *(vr)*

p. 115: 'When my father shuffled off this mortal coil':
In the original the French colloquial expression for dying – *'quitter le plancher des vaches'* – leads in as if naturally to the indigestible 'blanquette de veau'. I couldn't find a good English colloquial equivalent, so I decided to go for Shakespeare again, and a half-rhyme. *(sw)*

p. 117: 'They bring their teacher hearts...':
ll. 1-2: The English name for the plant *'l'amour en cage'* is 'Chinese lantern'. In the end I chose to lose the original walnut

metaphor to make space for this one, which seemed more crucial. *(sw)*

p. 121: 'So I's the host...':
l. 6: A straightforward translation of the original French would read 'Rouzeau with network dentist with time of sadness', but the wordplay here seemed to me more crucial. *(sw)*

p. 123: 'A great fat budgie-squawk...':
l. 10: 'Agagax': Agagax is a baby gangster character chased by Supermatou in the cartoon by illustrator Jean-Claude Poirier for *Pif Gadget* in the 70's. *(vr)*

p. 125: 'When I'd fill up the fridge...':
l. 3: 'these great burgers': at the 'Hot Croissant' they used to serve 'lollies' made of meat stuffed into pieces of baguette. *(vr)*

p. 127: 'Won't write a word today...':
See note to p. 101, 'Not far from really understanding...' *(vr)* The 'yes' in the last line is in English in the original.

p. 129: 'No I'm not back...':
l. 13: 'guessed': word and context seemed to me to invite this playful mis-spelling. *(sw)*

p. 129: 'Asters or asterisks...':
l. 2: 'trike inserted to extend the racing-bike iage, and for the rhyme. *(sw)*
l. 6: 'sty of china pigs': In French, recorders have beaks, but in English they don't, of course – so I decided to change the metaphor. *(sw)*
l. 7: 'air-ghostess': this was a happy typo, which made us both laugh, and which we were unanimous in our decision to leave in. I've mentioned it in my translator's introduction. *(sw)*

p. 131: 'Each day these perfect strangers...':
'I am afraid of a bee as I am of a kiss': the first two lines, disordered, of Verlaine's poem, 'A Poor Young Shepherd'. *(vr)*

p. 131: 'Before you leave the train…':

All my gratitude to the SNCF in general, and to the railway employee who came out with the wonderful jumble of words reproduced in l. 2 [of the original] in particular. *(vr)*

VALÉRIE ROUZEAU was born in 1967 in Burgundy, France and now lives in Nevers. She has published fourteen poetry titles, including *Pas revoir* (le dé bleu, 1999), *Va où* (Le temps qu'il fait, 2002) and more recently *Quand Je Me Deux* (Le temps qu'il fait, 2009) and *Vrouz* (La table ronde, 2012).

She has also published volumes translated from Sylvia Plath, William Carlos Williams, Ted Hughes and the photographer Duane Michals. She has been the editor of a little review of poetry for children (from 5 to 117 years old) called *dans la lune*, and lives mainly by her pen through public readings, poetry workshops in schools, radio broadcasts and translation.

Cold Spring in Winter, the English translation of *Pas revoir,* was short-listed for the International Griffin Prize for Poetry in 2010. Her most recent collection, *Vrouz,* was the winner of France's Apollinaire Prize in 2012.

SUSAN WICKS, poet and novelist, was born in Kent, England, in 1947. She read French at the universities of Hull and Sussex, and wrote a D. Phil. thesis on André Gide. She has lived and worked in France, Ireland and America and has taught at the University of Dijon, University College Dublin and the University of Kent.

She is the author of six collections of poetry including *House of Tongues* (2011), *Singing Underwater* (1992), which won the Aldeburgh Poetry Festival Prize, and *The Clever Daughter* (1996), which was short-listed for both the T. S. Eliot and Forward Prizes. She was one of the Poetry Society's 'New Generation Poets' in 1994. She is also the author of a short experimental memoir, *Driving My Father* (1995), and three novels, the most recent of which, *A Place to Stop,* came out in 2012.

Cold Spring in Winter (2010), her translation of Valérie Rouzeau's first major collection, *Pas revoir,* was short-listed both for the Oxford-Weidenfeld Prize for Literary Translation and the International Griffin Prize for Poetry, and won that year's Scott Moncrieff Prize for Translation from French.

Arc Publications
publishes translated poetry in bilingual editions
in the following series:

'VISIBLE POETS'
Series Editor: Jean Boase-Beier

ARC TRANSLATIONS
Series Editor: Jean Boase-Beier

'ARC CLASSICS'
NEW TRANSLATIONS OF GREAT POETS OF THE PAST
Series Editor: Jean Boase-Beier

ARC ANTHOLOGIES IN TRANSLATION
Series Editor: Jean Boase-Beier

'NEW VOICES FROM EUROPE & BEYOND'
anthology series
Series Editor: Alexandra Büchler

Full details of the titles in these series
can be found on the
Arc Publications website at
www.arcpublications.co.uk